Charles Spurgeon [...]
tion of superlative [...] mastery
of the English language, a keen mind and memory, sound theological instincts, and fearless devotion to the truth. He preached
a timeless message with extraordinary clarity and conviction.
His sermons are therefore as rich and edifying as when they were
first delivered. If you're not reading Spurgeon's sermons, you
need to do a better job of redeeming the time.

– **Phil Johnson**

I like to read Spurgeon because his fierce passion for biblical truth
comes through so clearly, even in print. I greatly admire his commitment to sound doctrine, his hatred of heresy, his passion for
souls, and his knowledge of Scripture. But more than anything
else, I appreciate his deep love for Christ. All of it is contagious.

– **John MacArthur**

TEN ESSENTIAL SERMONS OF CHARLES SPURGEON

TEN ESSENTIAL SERMONS OF CHARLES SPURGEON

INTRODUCTION BY TOM NETTLES

FREE GRACE PRESS

Published by

Free Grace Press
3900 Dave Ward Dr., Ste. 1900
Conway, AR 72034
(501) 214-9663
email: support@freegracepress.com
website: www.freegracepress.com

Printed in the United States of America

Scripture quotations are from the ESV® Bible (The Holy Bible, English Standard Version®), copyright © 2001 by Crossway, a publishing ministry of Good News Publishers. Used by permission. All rights reserved.

Scripture quotations marked (NKJV) taken from the New King James Version®. Copyright © 1982 by Thomas Nelson. Used by permission. All rights reserved.

Scripture quotations marked (KJV) taken from the King James Version. Public domain.

Cover design by Scott Schaller

ISBN: 978-1-952599-43-9

For additional Reformed Baptist titles, please email us for a free list or see our website at the above address.

Contents

Introduction

Charles Haddon Spurgeon had no peer in the theological density of his sermons. At the same time, he had no peer in their simplicity. He looked at truth, to which Christ came to bear witness and embody, as the pathway not only for altering the mind but for shaping the affections. These ten sermons exemplify this pattern of deep doctrine, simple but elegant and engaging presentation, and a call to faith and love.

In the first sermon of this volume, Spurgeon explains the way of salvation and its effects in the life of believers. He prefaces the sermon by saying, "It is proper, then, for the preacher to address his hearers sometimes as if they were totally ignorant of his message and tell it to them as a new thing." He always aimed at simplicity. Simplicity, however, did not mean lack of depth or careless and unstudied presentation of truth. The depths of insight, biblical knowledge, and doctrinal synthesis that support his clear explanation of sin, condemnation, forgiveness, justification, and increasing freedom from the ravages of corruption are obvious. They show knowledge of the Bible, theological literature, historical development of doctrine, and unvarnished commitment to biblical orthodoxy. Spurgeon's plainness, simplicity, and urgently pursued clarity demonstrated the depth and thoroughness of his understanding and the intensity of his desire for the understanding of his auditory. His urgent and simple call for the sinner to believe did not serve as a reason to avoid predestination, election, the necessity of effectual call, an efficacious atonement for the elect, or the determination of God to preserve his elect, but these doctrines were announced in service of his evangelistic call. Nothing could be more honoring to God and thoroughly humbling to sinners that the realization of

1

absolute dependence on grace. Spurgeon hammered that truth home with unrelenting insistence while not diminishing the clarity with which he assured the lost that if they will call on the name of the Lord, they will be saved.

The second sermon emphasizes the Christian calling of fishing for men. He did not like to isolate the central task of Christian ministry to those who were pastors of churches. Spurgeon also looked upon the believers in his congregation as among the *cleros*, those called to ministry, and saw them as the evangelistic arm of the church: "I think I may say to every person whom I am addressing—if you are saved, the work is but half done until you are employed to bring others to Christ!" They should examine the way Jesus drew their own souls to salvation, look at his method and passion in the gospels, and learn from Him to be such fishermen. "Follow Me," Jesus said. "Watch how he does the work and so learn how to do it yourself," Spurgeon urged. "A Christian man should be bound apprentice to Jesus to learn the trade of a savior!"

The third sermon is a beautiful exposition of the faith of the dying thief. Spurgeon's synthesis of doctrine is evident in this sermon as is his penchant for striking and apt images. Though Spurgeon was certain that anyone who believes at any stage of life or in any situation will assuredly be saved, he did not use this narrative as an encouragement for late or death-bed conversion. Rather, he saw in the event a concentrated manifestation of all the elements of gospel knowledge, repentance, faith, assurance, and courage in the face of opposition. In speaking of the depth of the thief's repentance, Spurgeon noted, "As I have often told you, I suspect the faith that is not born as a twin with repentance; but there is no room for suspicion in the case of this penitent confessor." Noting the intensity of the saving grace experienced by the thief finding forgiveness, immediate assurance, and glory in paradise within a few hours, Spurgeon made the comparison, "He did not take any one of us from nature to grace, and from grace to glory, in a day. We have had to wait a good while."

The fourth sermon considers the theme of "Songs in the Night" from Elihu's speech in Job. Spurgeon explores the theme of night as the times of difficulty into which Christians often enter. "Man is a little world in that man resembles the world in almost everything. And if the world has its night, so man has his night." He looked at songs in the night, considering their "source, their content, their excellence, and their uses." We should not be surprised that night comes to us, for Christians realize that they are "not so poor as [we] deserve to be." All that we have, we have of mercy. In this sermon, Spurgeon makes a strong social comment about the low wages of the weavers of Spitalsfield. He showed that the Christians among them had little expectation of either justice or mercy from men but looked to the future for their song when Jesus would come. Our songs finally must be songs of praise to Jesus. "He who sings a song to Christ in the night sings the best song in all the world, for he sings from the heart." The song in the night also is the best apologetic for the truth of Christianity. "Try and sing in the night, Christian, for that is one of the best arguments in all the world for Christian faith." Spurgeon did not recommend disputing with unbelievers but in proclaiming the truth of God with a mission. Believe and be saved; remain in unbelief and be damned. "I tell you," Spurgeon insisted, "we may preach fifty thousand sermons to prove the gospel, but we will not prove it half so well as you will through singing in the night." The night will come too soon for unbelievers who will have no song of praise and gratitude but only groans of despair.

The fifth sermon looks to Jesus's word about God's provision for ravens. He turns it into an evangelistic sermon and an encouragement for those seeking salvation. Ravens compare nothing in value to men, image-bearers of God. "And do you think that God will hear so low and so mean a creature as a raven, and yet not hear you, when you are one of those he formed in his own image?" Their croaks and cries out of simple physical need elicit God's care, "and will he not answer you, poor trembling children of men, who are seeking his face and favor through Christ Jesus?" Spurgeon never shirked the evangelist's duty of sincere and earnest affection for the souls of his hearers. "I long, tonight, to give you some comfort and encouragement," he pledged; "I want to urge you to cry yet more vehemently. Come to the cross and lay hold of it, and vow that you will never leave its shadow till you find the gift your soul covets." If their desires conformed to the gifts found in the gospel, they could be confident of being heard. "You know what you want—peace and pardon. You know that you need Jesus, his precious blood, his perfect righteousness." If God's answers the raven's chattering and indistinct cry for its mean sustenance, "don't you think he will also hear the rational and expressive prayer of a poor, needy, guilty soul who is crying unto him, 'God be merciful to me a sinner'?" Spurgeon takes issue both with the Arminians and the "Ultra-Calvinists" in this message and shows his appreciation for Andrew Fuller. The ultras took issue with Spurgeon's attempt to teach children that they ought to pray, calling it "rank Arminianism" and "Fullerism." Spurgeon considered the title "so honorable that I could heartily have thanked them for appending it to what I had advanced." Spurgeon closes this sermon with an extended encouragement for seekers and a relentless series of arguments to convince them of God's truthfulness in promising forgiveness and salvation for those who call on Him.

The sixth sermon, "The Shameful Sufferer," probes the astounding phenomenon of the substitutionary death of the Son of God. Spurgeon shows the power, beauty, and the simplicity of his rhetorical abilities in this effort to explore the unfathomable. Spurgeon has pungent words and biblical examples about the power of shame and then relates that human dread to the shameful suffering of Christ. "But Christ who was more than noble—matchlessly noble, something more than of a royal race—for him to be shamed and mocked must have been dreadful, indeed!" This theme brought forth some of the most emotionally gripping analogies and images that ever came from the mouth and irrepressible vocabulary and imagination of the man justly called the Prince of Preachers. Orthodoxy in Christ's person and the offices of his work is set forth concerning the shame endured by the Savior. Spurgeon gives rightful recognition to the desire of Jesus to honor the Father by his death, but he pours out his homiletic talent to make the point that his motive was the salvation of his enemies—his elect, his church, yes, but nevertheless, his hateful enemies. "The great motive, then, with Christ, in enduring all this, was that he might save us!" Given such a shameful death of such a savior for such sinners, shall we not gladly suffer for Him?

The seventh of these sermons looks to the issue of "soul winning." To this preeminent calling of the Christian, Spurgeon gave himself, and to inculcate the zeal, content, encouragement, and expectation of soul-winning in his congregation constantly infused his sermons. Using a text from Proverbs 11:30 concerning the fruit of the righteous and the winning of souls, Spurgeon dealt with those two points. There must be a righteous life that flows naturally from the heart of faith to prepare the way for soul-winning. "Dear brothers and sisters, we must take care that our religion is more and more a matter of outgrowth from our souls." Unrighteous living, no matter how smoothly covered with external acts of apparent piety, speaks of one who knows not the righteousness of Christ. A cheat in the market is a cheat in his religion. "A false profession is one of the worst of lies since it brings the utmost dishonor upon Christ and his people. The fruit of the *righteous* is *righteousness.*"

Winning involves wooing like a suitor does a future bride or a military officer plans for winning a battle; it is like winning a fortune with planning, sacrifice, shrewdness, and long hours. "We have to go in for winning souls, with the same ardor and concentration of our faculties as old Astor of New York went in to build up that fortune of so many millions." It is like training to win a race, and we will not win souls if we do not imitate the devoted athlete in this. Considering all the possible things to which a person could devote his wisdom and energy, Spurgeon said, "My dear friend, nothing will equal in enjoyment, in usefulness, in honor, and in lasting recompense than the giving yourself up to the winning of souls!" Spurgeon defended orthodox faith in the face of heresy and various kinds of sectarianism as well as anybody and with great zeal and courage. Yet, he asserted, "It is a very good thing to contend earnestly for the faith once delivered to the saints, but I do not think I should like to say in my last account, 'Lord, I have lived to fight the Romanists and the State church and to put down the various erroneous sects, but I never led a sinner to the cross.'" He was as eloquent naturally and from close study as any pulpiteer in England, yet he would say, "Let eloquence be flung to the dogs rather than souls lost!"

The theme of the cross comes again in sermon 8. How does a person crucified as a blasphemer, a felon, and a rebel draw men to himself? Notorious criminals are put away from public view and are not paraded forth as attractions for public consumption. Yet Jesus put the center of gravity of his attracting power in the very ignominious instrument of his punishment: "If I be lifted up." Spurgeon focused on this then by asking, In what way does the Savior on the cross have such a compelling attraction? He pointed first to its manifestation of eternal and immutable love. "If I were asked the secret of the attracting power of the crucified Savior, I would answer that it is invincible love." Then he would add to that attribute the Savior himself and point to its effects in the life of the one drawn. "He draws men by the wonderful rest that his death provides for men"— not this world of sin and destruction and hate and malicious relations but heaven in the company of God, saints, and holy angels; not hell and the presence of devils and divine wrath but heaven and the unending, inexhaustible joy of God's presence. The drawn ones are freed from guilt and have the vow of God to bring them to the place wherein dwells righteousness. "When I see Jesus die, I perceive that from now on divine justice is on the sinner's side. How can the Lord God punish the same offense twice—first the Substitute and then the men for whom that Substitute has bled?"

In addition, the uplifted Savior attracts "when we see the change he works in men." Drunkards become sober; harlots become pure; thieves become honest; abusers become tender caregivers. Spurgeon believed that, given all the circumstances of this death, the drawing power "lies much in his sufferings themselves." More even than in the powerful witness of martyrs who became seed for the church, by the agonies of Jesus "men's affections are moved and their hearts enthralled." Only the Holy Spirit has final power to draw rebels to Christ, but he does this by empowering instruments. This drawing often develops gradually; often it is done secretly until fully ripened. But if it be a drawing unto true faith, it is done effectually. This means that none are born converted nor made a Christian at the font. They must be drawn so that they come to know and believe. Such is the perversity of human sin, that even with all these elements of drawing power and drawing instruments, "men will not come to Christ unless he draws them."

Fittingly, after the lifting up, this book of sermons moves to the taking down and the burial. Spurgeon draws the reader with beauty, tenderness, skill, and pious zeal for us to "come see the place where the Lord lay." Preached on Easter morning, the sermon looked with wonder at the place where God in the flesh was laid to rest for a short time after having accomplished the most powerful and loving feat in the history of the world and as a fulfillment of eternal counsels—the reconciliation of God and man. He saw it as a place of quietness, beauty, and rest. When the Christian says, "I am sick of this tiring and trying life. My frame is weary, my soul is mad to repose herself a while," Spurgeon points to the empty tomb and prescribes it as "a sweet resting spot, a withdrawing room for your soul, where you may brush your garments from the dust of earth and muse a while in peace."

Spurgeon wanted the contemplation of the tomb to reach into the emotions of his hearers with transforming power. "I love a religion that consists, in a great measure, of emotion," he admitted. "Now, if I had power, like a master I would touch the strings of your hearts and fetch a glorious tune of solemn music from them, for this is a deeply solemn place into which I have conducted you." He would like for them to experience "emotions of deep sorrow," indeed, to "feel deep grief" for their "deliverer lost his life in the attempt" to save them. He also wanted them to view the tomb with "joy and gladness," for it was empty, unspoiled, uncorrupted, but rather, sanctified by the body that had lain there. The tomb of the perfectly righteous man who died because of sin should instruct all who look upon it that death will come. It cannot be avoided or postponed, and after that, the judgment. Looking at the place where the Lord lay also will teach of Christ's divinity, our acquittal, and the certainty of resurrection.

The final sermon in this collection gives a picture of the glorious state of the saints in heaven, even now as sin and corruption still strut on the earth. It is filled with comforting and strong insight as the perfect satisfaction that redeemed spirits have in the wisdom and providence of God, even as they ask fervently, "How long?" While the redeemed glory in the sovereignty of grace and the wisdom of God in his eternal counsels, they know unflinchingly the absolute justice of the condemnation of those who remained in an unbelieving state, unwashed by the blood of the Lamb: "Your damnation," so Spurgeon announced, "will be as just as it will be sure."

The effort to isolate ten influential sermons from a preacher who preached thousands of such sermons is daunting. These sermons, however, succeed in illustrating Spurgeon's doctrine, his evangelistic commitment, the beauty of his language, the manner in which a biblical text suggests a subject, and his passion for the glory of the triune God and the eternal well-being of souls.

Tom J. Nettles

A Simple Sermon for Seeking Souls

No. 140, Music Hall, Royal Surrey Gardens, London, England
July 12, 1857

For "everyone who calls on the name
of the Lord will be saved."
– Romans 10:13

It has been said by a notable theologian that many of us preachers presume our hearts know more than they do. "Very often," says this divine, "there are those in the congregation who are totally unacquainted with the great science of divinity. They are complete strangers to the whole system of grace and salvation." It is proper, then, for the preacher to address his hearers sometimes as if they were totally ignorant of his message and tell it to them as a new thing. "For," says this good man, "it is better to suppose too little knowledge and so to explain the thing clearly than to suppose too much and, thus, to let the ignorant escape without a word of instruction."

With this in mind, I will assume that some of my congregation are totally unacquainted with the great plan of salvation. I will try in the simplest words that human lips can put together to tell the story of how the lost can be saved, according to the words of my text, by calling on the name of the Lord.

Well then, we must begin at the beginning. And we must first tell our hearers that because our text talks of men being saved, it implies that men need saving. If men had been as God created them, they would not need saving. In the garden, Adam needed no salvation. Adam was perfect, pure, clean, holy, and acceptable before God. He was our representative when he touched the forbidden fruit and ate of the tree of which God had said, "You shall not eat, for in the day that you eat of it you shall surely die" (Gen. 2:17). And it was only after Adam sinned against God that he needed a savior. And we, his offspring through his sin, are born into this world needing a savior as well.

We who are now present must not throw blame on Adam, for no man was ever damned for Adam's sin alone. Children dying in infancy are, without a doubt, saved by sovereign grace through the atonement that is in Christ Jesus. No sooner do they close their eyes to earth, being innocent of any actual sin, than they at once open them in the bliss of heaven. But you and I are not children. We need not talk of Adam's sins. We have our own sins for which to give an account, for God knows they are enough to condemn us.

Holy Scripture tells us that we have all sinned and come short of the glory of God. Moreover, our conscience bears witness to the same truth. We have all broken the commands of God. Consequently, God is bound in justice to punish us for the sins we have committed.

Now, my brethren, because you and I have broken the divine law and are subject to the divine wrath, we stand in need of mercy. Every one of us, if we would be happy, and if we would dwell in heaven with God forever, must be saved.

But there is great confusion in the minds of men of what it means to be saved. Allow me, then, to say that salvation means two things. First, it means escaping from the *punishment* of sin; second, it means escaping from the *enslavement* of sin.

God saves in two ways: he finds a sinner who has broken his law, and he says, "I forgive you. I will not punish you. I have punished Christ instead of you. You shall be saved." But that is only half the work of Christ. He next says, "I will not let you go on sinning as you have been doing. I will give you a new heart, which shall subdue your evil habits. So, as you have been the slave of sin, you shall be free to serve Me. Come away—you are not going to serve that master of yours anymore. You must leave that demon. I will have you to be My child, My servant. You may reply, 'I cannot do so.' Come, I will give you grace to do it—I will give you grace to break off drunkenness, grace to renounce swearing, grace to give up Sabbath-breaking; I will give you grace to run in the ways of my commandments and to find obedience to be a delightful road." Salvation, then, I say, consists of two things—deliverance from the habit of living in enmity with God and deliverance from the punishment that is tied to transgression.

The great subject of this morning, which I will attempt to dwell on in plain language, is *how men may be saved*. That is the ultimate question of life. Let us remember what it means to be saved. It is to be made Christians, to have new thoughts, new minds, new hearts, and then, it is to have a new home forever at God's right hand in glory. How may you be saved? "What must I do to be saved?" is a cry springing from many lips this morning. The answer of my text is this: "For 'everyone who calls on the name of the Lord will be saved.'"

First, I will try to explain the text—*explanation*. Second, I will try to clear the text from some popular errors about salvation—that will be *refutation*. Third, I will press the usefulness of my text on your minds—*exhortation*. Thus, my three points are explanation, refutation, and exhortation. You will remember the points, and may God impress them upon your minds!

Explanation

What is here meant by calling on the name of the Lord? I tremble at this very moment as I try to explain my text, for I feel it is quite easy to darken words without knowledge. Too many times preachers render Scripture dark by their explanations instead of making it clearer. Many preachers have been like painted windows that shut out the light rather than admitting it.

Nothing puzzles and tries my mind more than the question, What is faith? What is believing? What is calling on the name of the Lord? To answer this question, I have turned to my concordance to seek out the passages where the same word is employed. As far as I can judge, I may state from the authority of Scripture that the word *call* signifies worship. I might translate it thus: "Everyone who *worships* God shall be saved." But we must first explain the word *worship* if we are to understand the Scriptural significance of it.

To call on the name of the Lord means to *worship* God. You will find in the book of Genesis that "when men began to multiply on the face of the earth, they began to *call* on the name of the Lord." That is, they began to worship God. They built altars in his name; they certified their belief in the sacrifice that was to come by offering a typical sacrifice. They bowed their knee in prayer, they lifted their voice in sacred song, and they cried, "Great is Jehovah, Creator, Preserver. Let him be praised."

Now "everyone" includes whoever that may be in the wide, wide world who is enabled by grace to worship God in God's way. If you worship him by a Mediator, having faith in the atonement of the cross, if you worship him by humble prayer and hearty praise, then your worship is a proof that you are saved. You could not worship without grace in your heart. And your faith and grace are proofs that you will have glory.

Everyone, then, in lowly devotion, on the green grass that lies beneath the spreading branches of a tree, in God's house or out of it, who may worship God with a pure heart fervently, looking for acceptance through the atonement of Christ and meekly casting himself on the mercy of God, will be saved. So stands the promise.

But lest anyone should run away with a mistaken idea of what worship is, we must explain a little further. The word *call* in holy Scripture also signifies *prayer.* You remember the case of Elijah: after the prophets of Baal were unable to get rain from their false gods, Elijah said, "I will call on God"—that is to say, "I will pray to God that he may send rain." Now, prayer is a sure sign of divine life within. Everyone who prays to God through Christ, with a sincere heart, will be saved.

Oh, I can remember how this text cheered my soul. I felt the weight of sin, and I did not know the Savior. I thought God would blast me with his wrath and smite me with his hot displeasure! From chapel to chapel I went to hear the Word preached, but never a gospel sentence did I hear. But this one text preserved me. Without this text I believe I would have been driven to suicide. It was this sweet word, "Everyone who calls on the name of the Lord will be saved."

Well, I thought, I cannot believe on Christ as I could wish, but I know I can call on his name. If I am ever lost, I will plead that promise, "Everyone who calls on the name of the Lord will be saved." I did call on Christ that night. Will God cast me away now? I did plead his promise. I did lift up my heart in prayer. Can God be just and damn my soul to hell?

But mark that sweet thought: prayer is the forerunner of salvation. Sinner, you cannot pray and perish, for prayer and perishing are two things that never go together. I ask you not what your prayer is. It may be a groan, it may be a tear, a wordless prayer, or a prayer in broken English that is harsh to the ear, but if it is a prayer from the innermost heart, you will be saved—or else this promise is a lie. As surely as you pray, whoever you may be, whatever you may have done, and whatever the transgressions you may have committed, yet if from your heart you have learned to pray, then you cannot perish with God's breath in you, "for everyone who calls on the name of the Lord will be saved!"

But the word *call* signifies a little more. It signifies *trust*. A person cannot call on the name of the Lord unless he trusts in that name. We must have reliance on the name of Christ or else we have not called on him rightly. Hear me, then, poor sinner. You who have come here this morning aware of your guilt and awakened to your danger, here is your remedy. Christ Jesus is the Son of God. He became a man; he was "born of the virgin Mary, suffered under Pontius Pilate, was crucified, died, and was buried." He did this to save sinners such as you. Will you believe this? Will you trust your soul to it? Will you say, "Sink or swim, Christ Jesus is my hope; and if I perish, then I will perish with my arms around his cross, crying, 'Nothing in my hands I bring, simply to the cross I cling'"?

Poor soul, if you can do that, you will be saved. Come now, no good works of your own are needed. No sacraments are needed. All that is asked of you is that which he gives you. You are nothing— will you take Christ to be everything? Come. You are dirty—will you be washed? Will you go down on your knees and cry, "Lord, have mercy on me, a sinner, not for anything I have done, or can do, but for his dear sake whose blood streamed from his hands and feet, in whom I alone trust"? The solid pillars of the universe will totter rather than you should perish. Heaven should weep a vacant throne and an extinguished Godhead rather than the promise be violated. He that trusts in Christ, calling on his name, will be saved.

But once more, and then I think I will have given you the whole Scripture meaning of this—calling on the name of the Lord signifies *professing his name.* You remember what Ananias said to Saul, later called Paul: "Arise and be baptized, and wash away your sins, calling on the name of the Lord"? Now, sinner, will you be obedient to Christ's Word? His Word says, "He that believes, and is *immersed,* shall be saved."

Mark how I have translated the word. The King James Version does not translate it. I dare not be unfaithful to my knowledge of God's Word. If it means sprinkle, let our brethren translate it "sprinkle." But they dare not do that; they know they have nothing in all classical language that would ever justify them in doing that, and they have not the impudence to attempt it. But I dare translate it, "He that believes, and is *immersed,* shall be saved."

And though immersion is nothing, God requires those who believe to be immersed to make a profession of their belief. I repeat, immersion is nothing. It is the profession of salvation. God requires that everyone who trusts in the Savior be immersed.

The Savior was immersed to fulfill all righteousness. As Jesus went meekly down from Jordan's shore to be immersed beneath the waves, so let every believer be baptized in his name.

Now some of you draw back from the thought of making a profession. "No," you say, "we will believe and be secret Christians." Hear this: "If any man be ashamed of me, and of my words in this generation; of him will I be ashamed, when I shall come in the glory of my Father, with all his holy angels."

I will repeat a truism: none of you has ever known a secret Christian. For if you knew a man to be a Christian, it could not be a secret; for if it had been a secret, how did you come to know it? Then, as you never knew a secret Christian, you are not justified in believing there ever is such a one. You must come out and make a profession.

What would Her Majesty think of her soldiers if they should swear their loyalty yet say, "Your Majesty, we prefer not to wear these regimentals. Let us wear the dress of civilians! We are honest men, but we do not care to stand in your ranks and be acknowledged as your soldiers. We had rather slip into the enemy's camp, and into your camps too, and not wear anything that would mark us as being your soldiers!" Ah! some of you do the same with Christ. You are going to be secret Christians, are you? Do you desire to slip into the devil's camp, and into Christ's camp, but be acknowledged by none?

Well, you may be willing to take the chance, but I would not want to risk it. It is a solemn threatening: "Of him will I be ashamed when I come in the glory of my Father, and all his holy angels with me!" It is a solemn thing, I say, when Christ says, "Except a man take up his cross and follow me, he cannot be my disciple." Now, then, I charge every sinner here in whom God has awakened to feel his need of a Savior to obey the command of Christ. Obey not only in this point but obey in every other point as well.

Hear the way of salvation: worship, prayer, faith, and profession. And the profession, if men would be obedient, if they would follow the Bible, must be done in Christ's way—by a baptism in water, in the name of the Father, of the Son, and of the Holy Spirit. God requires this. Men are saved without baptism (as baptism does not save); however, if men would be saved, they must not be disobedient. Inasmuch as God gives a command, it is mine to enforce it. Jesus said, "Go into all the world and proclaim the gospel to the whole creation. Whoever believes and is baptized will be saved, but whoever does not believe will be condemned."

Refutation

There are some popular errors regarding salvation that need correcting. My text says, "For everyone who calls on the name of the Lord will be saved."

Now, one idea that conflicts with my text is this, *that a priest or a minister is absolutely necessary to assist men in salvation.* That idea is current in other places besides the Romish Church. There are many—alas! too many—who make a gospel minister as much their priest as the Catholic makes his priest his helper. There are many who imagine that salvation cannot be accomplished except in some indefinable and mysterious way connected with the minister of the gospel.

Hear, then, if you have never seen a minister, if you had never heard the voice of the bishop or elder, yet if you call on the name of the Lord, your salvation would be just as sure without one as with one.

Men cannot call upon a God they do not know. The necessity of a preacher lies in telling others the way of salvation, for how can they hear without a preacher, and how can they believe in him of whom they have not heard? But the preacher's office goes no further than proclaiming the message. After we have told others the way, the Holy Spirit must apply it. We can go no further.

Oh, take care of priestcraft, take care of mancraft, of ministercraft, and of clergycraft. All God's people are clergy. We are all God's *cleros.* We are all his clergy if we have been saved and anointed with the Holy Spirit. There never should have been a distinction between clergy and laity.

We are all clergy who love the Lord Jesus Christ. And you are as much fit to preach the gospel, if God has given you the ability and has called you to the work by his Spirit, as any man alive. No priestly hand or ordination of men is necessary. We stand on the rights of manhood to speak what we believe. And next to that, we stand on the call of God's Spirit in the heart that bids us to testify of his truth.

But, brethren, neither Paul nor an angel from heaven nor Apollos or Cephas can help you in salvation. Salvation is not of man, neither by men. Neither pope nor archbishop nor bishop nor priest nor minister nor anyone else can impart grace to you. We must each go ourselves to the fountainhead, pleading this promise: "For everyone who calls on the name of the Lord will be saved."

If I were shut up in the mines of Siberia, without access to a gospel minster, and if I called on the name of Christ, the road is just as straight without the minister as with him. The path to heaven is just as clear from the wilds of Africa and from the dens of the prison house as it is from the sanctuary of God.

Nevertheless, for edification, all Christians love the ministry, though not for salvation. Though neither in priest nor preacher do they trust, yet the Word of God is sweet to them, and "How beautiful are the feet of those who preach the good news!" (Rom. 10:15).

Another common error is that salvation comes to us in a dream. Some of you do not know the extent to which this error prevails. I happen to know it. It is believed by many that if you dream of the Lord in your sleep, you will be saved. If you can see him on the cross or if you think you see some angels or if you dream that God says to you, "You are forgiven," all is well. There are those who believe if you do not have a dream such as this, you cannot be saved.

Now, if this were true, the sooner we all begin to eat opium, the better, because there is nothing that makes people dream so much as that. And the best advice I could give would be this: let every minister distribute opium liberally, and then his people would all dream themselves into heaven. But out with such rubbish; there is nothing in it.

How can dreams, the disordered fabrics of a wild imagination, be the means of salvation? You know Rowland Hill's good answer? I must quote it in default of having any better answer myself. When a woman pleaded that she was saved because she dreamed, he said, "Well, my good woman, it is very nice to have good dreams when you are asleep; but I want to see how you act when you are awake. If your conduct is not consistent with religion when you are awake, I do not give a snap of the finger for your dreams."

Ah, I do marvel that any person should go to such a depth of ignorance as to tell me the stories that I have heard about dreams. Poor dear creatures, when they were sound asleep, they saw the gates of heaven opened, and a white angel came and washed their sins away, and then they saw that they were pardoned. Since then they have never had a doubt or a fear. It is time that you should begin to doubt, for if that is all the hope you have, it is a poor one. Remember it is, "For everyone who calls on the name of the Lord will be saved," not whosoever dreams about him.

Dreams may do some good. Sometimes people have been frightened out of their senses by them; and they were better out of their senses than they were in them. They did more mischief when they were in their senses than when they were out of them. In this sense, dreams did them some good. Though some people have become alarmed by dreams, to trust them is to trust in a shadow, and it is to build your hopes on bubbles that need only a puff of wind to burst them into nothingness.

Oh! remember, you need no vision, no marvelous appearance. If you have had a vision or a dream, you need not despise it. Though they may have benefitted you, do not trust them. But if you have had none, remember that it is the mere calling on God's name by which the promise is secured.

And now, once again, there are others, a very good sort of people too, who have been laughing while I was talking about dreams. Now it is our turn to laugh at them. There are some people who think they must have some wonderful experience or feelings, or else they cannot be saved. Some feel they must have some extraordinary thoughts such as they never had before, or else they cannot be saved.

A woman once asked me about being admitted to church membership. So, I asked her whether she had ever had a change of heart. "Oh, yes, sir, such a change as you know," she said. "I felt it across the chest particularly, sir. When I was a praying one day, I felt as if I did not know what was wrong with me—I felt so different. And when I went to the chapel, sir, one night, I came away and felt so different from what I felt before, so light."

"Yes," I said, "light-headed, my dear soul, that is what you felt, but nothing more, I am afraid."

The good woman was sincere enough. She thought it was all right with her because something had affected her lungs or in some way stirred her physical frame.

"No," I hear some of you say, "people cannot be so stupid as this." I assure you that if you could read the hearts of this present congregation, you would find there are hundreds here who have no better hope of heaven than that.

I am dealing with a very popular objection. "I thought," said one addressing me one day, "I thought when I was in the garden that Christ could take my sins away just as easily as he could move the clouds. Do you know, sir, in a moment or two the clouds were all gone and the sun was shining. I thought to myself, The Lord is blotting out my sin." Such a ridiculous thought as that, you say, cannot occur often. I tell you, it does, very frequently indeed. People often think such nonsense is a manifestation of divine grace in their hearts.

Now, the only feeling I want to have is this: I want to feel that I am a sinner and that Christ is my Savior. You may keep your visions and ecstasies and raptures to yourselves. The only feeling I desire to have is deep repentance and humble faith. And if, poor sinner, you have got that, you are saved.

Why, some of you believe that before you can be saved there

must be a kind of electric shock, some very wonderful thing that is to go all through you from head to foot. Now hear this: "The word is near you, in your mouth and in your heart," and "if you confess with your mouth that Jesus is Lord and believe in your heart that God raised him from the dead, you will be saved" (Rom. 10:8–9). What do you want with all this nonsense of dreams and supernatural thoughts? All that is needed is that I should come as a guilty sinner and cast myself on Christ. That done, the soul is safe, and all the visions in the universe could not make it safer.

And now, I have one more error to try to rectify. This error exists among poor people. I have visited some of them and know it to be true. There are some here, and I will speak to them, among the poor and uneducated, who believe that, somehow or another, salvation is connected with learning to read and write. You smile, perhaps, but I know it. Often has a poor woman said, "Oh! sir, it is not good to be poor and ignorant like us. There is no hope for me, sir. I cannot read. Do you know, sir, I don't know a letter? I think if I could read a bit, I might be saved. But ignorant as I am, I do not know how to call on him, for I have no understanding, sir."

I have found this in the country districts too, among people who might learn to read if they liked. And all people, unless they are lazy, can learn to read. And yet they sit down in cold indifference about their salvation. They think that the person who reads, such as a clerk, can be saved. They think the squire who said, "Amen," so well could be saved for he knows a great deal and has a lot of books in his library—but that they cannot be saved because they did not know anything.

Now, have I one such poor creature here? I will speak plainly to you. My poor friend, you do not need to know much to go to heaven. I would advise you to know as much as you can. Do not be slow in your desire to learn. But in regard to going to heaven, the way is so plain that even "the wayfaring man, though a fool, shall not err therein."

Do you feel that you have been guilty, that you have broken God's commandments, that you have not kept his Sabbath, that you have taken his name in vain, that you have not loved your neighbor as yourself or your God with all your heart? Well, if you feel it, Christ died for such as you. He died on the cross and was punished in your place. And Christ tells you to believe it. If you want to hear more about it, come to the house of God and listen, and we will try to lead you to greater understanding. But remember, all you need to know to get to heaven is the two things that begin with *s*—sin and Savior.

Do you feel your sin? Christ is your Savior. Trust him. Pray to him, and as sure as I am talking to you now, you will one day be in heaven. I will tell you two prayers to pray. First, pray this prayer: "Lord, show me myself." That is an easy one for you. "Lord, show me myself; show me my heart; show me my guilt; show me my danger; Lord, show me myself." And, when you have prayed that prayer, and God has answered it (and remember, he hears prayer), then here is another prayer for you: "Lord, show me *Yourself*. Show me your work, your love, your mercy, your cross, and your grace." Pray that, and those are about the only prayers you need to pray to get to heaven. "Lord, show me myself," and "Lord, show me yourself."

You do not need to know much. You need not spell to get to heaven. You need not be able to speak English to get to heaven. The ignorant and unskilled in speech are welcome to the cross of Christ and salvation.

Excuse me for answering these popular errors. I answer them because they *are* popular, and popular among some who are present. Oh, men and women, hear the Word of God once more. "For 'everyone who calls on the name of the Lord will be saved.'" Man of eighty, child of eight, young man, maiden, rich, poor, literate, illiterate, to you is this preached in all its fullness and freeness, yes, to every creature under heaven. "Everyone"— and that shuts out none—"who calls on the name of the Lord will be saved."

Exhortation

My exhortation is, I entreat you by the name of God, believe the message that this day I declare from God's Word. Do not turn away from me because the message is simple. Do not reject it because I have chosen to preach it simply and plainly to the poor, but listen carefully again, "for 'everyone who calls on the name of the Lord will be saved.'" I beseech you to believe this.

Does it seem hard to believe? Nothing is too hard for the Most High. Do you say, "I have been so guilty, I cannot think God will save me"? Hear Jehovah speak: "My thoughts are not your thoughts; neither are my ways your ways. As high as the heavens are above the earth, so high are my thoughts above your thoughts, my ways above your ways." Do you say, "I am excluded; surely, you cannot mean that he would save me"? Listen! It says, "everyone"—and *everyone* is a great wide door that lets in big sinners. Oh, surely, if it says, "everyone," you are not excluded if you call on him.

And now come, I must plead with you, and I will use a few reasons to entice you to believe this truth. They shall be scriptural reasons. May God bless them to you, sinner.

If you call on Christ's name, you will be saved. I will tell you first, you will be saved because *you are elect.* No man ever called on Christ's name yet who was not elected. The doctrine of election, which puzzles many and frightens more, does not need to puzzle and frighten you. If you believe, you are elect. If you call on the name of Christ, you are elect. If you feel yourself to be a sinner and put your trust in Christ, you are elect.

Now, the elect will be saved, for there is no eternal death for them. God has predestinated them unto eternal life, and they shall never perish, neither shall any pluck them out of Christ's hands. God does not choose men and then cast them away. God does not elect them and then cast them into the pit.

Now, you are elect, or otherwise you could not have called. Your election is the cause of your calling. And because you have called and do call upon the name of God, you are God's elect. And neither death nor hell can ever erase your name from his Book. This is an omnipotent decree. Jehovah's will be done! His chosen must be saved, though earth and hell oppose, his strong hand shall break their ranks and lead his people through. You are one of these people. You shall at last stand before his throne and see his smiling face in glory because you are elect.

Now, another reason. If you will call on the name of the Lord, you shall be saved because *you have been redeemed.* Christ has bought you and paid for you. Christ poured out the hottest of his heart's blood to ransom you. Christ split his heart to buy your soul from wrath.

You are redeemed, but you do not know it. But I see the blood-mark on your brow. If you call on his name, though you are yet to have any comfort, Christ has called you his own. Ever since that day when he said, "It is finished," Christ has said, "My delight is in him, for I have bought him with my blood." Because you have been bought, you shall never perish. Not one of Jesus's blood-bought ones was ever lost yet.

Howl, howl, O hell, but in howling you cannot bring damnation to a redeemed soul. Out with that horrid doctrine that says men are damned who have been bought with blood. It is too diabolical for me to believe. I know what the Savior did—he redeemed.

And if he redeemed, then he redeemed those whom he redeemed from death and hell and wrath. I can never bring my mind to the unrighteous idea that Christ was punished for a man and that such a man will be punished again. I never could see how Christ could stand in a man's place and be punished for him and yet that man be punished again. No, since you call on God's name, there is proof that Christ is your ransom. Come, rejoice! If he was punished, God's justice cannot demand a double vengeance, first, at the bleeding Surety's hands and then again at yours.

Come, soul, put your hand upon the Savior's head, and say "Blessed Jesus, you were punished for me. Oh, God, I am not afraid of your vengeance. When my hand is on the atonement, smite, but you must smite me through your Son. Smite, if you will, but you cannot, for you have already smitten him, and you will not smite again for the same offense. What! Did Christ at one tremendous draught of love drink my damnation dry? And shall I be damned after that? God forbid!"

What! Shall God be unrighteous and forget the Redeemer's work for us and let the Savior's blood be shed in vain? Indeed, brethren, if you call on Christ, if you pray, if you believe, then you may be sure of salvation. If you believe, you are redeemed, and the redeemed will not perish.

Shall I tell you one more reason? Believe this truth; it must be true. For if you call upon the name of God, "in my Father's house," says Christ, "there are many mansions," and there is one there for you. Christ has prepared a house and a crown from before the foundation of the world for all those who believe. Come! Do you think Christ will prepare a house and not carry the inhabitant there? Will he make crowns and then loose the heads that are to wear them? God forbid!

Turn your eyes toward heaven. There is a seat there that must be filled and must be filled by you. There is a crown there that must be worn and must be worn by you. Oh! be of good cheer: heaven's preparation shall not be too abundant; he will make room for those who believe. And because he has made that room, those that believe will come there. Oh! I would to God that I might know that some soul could lay hold of this promise! Where are you? Are you standing away among the crowd there or sitting here in the body of the hall or in the upper gallery? Are you feeling your sins? Do you shed tears in secret on account of them? Do you lament your iniquities? Oh! take his promise: "For everyone"—sweet everyone!—"everyone who calls on the name of the Lord will be saved."

The devil says it is no use for you to call; you have been a drunkard. Tell him it says "everyone."

"No," says the evil spirit, "it is no use for you, for you have never been to hear a sermon or been in the house of God for the last ten years." Tell him it says "everyone."

"No," says Satan, "remember the sins from last night and how you have come up to the music hall stained with lust." Tell the devil it says "everyone" and that it is a foul falsehood of his that you can call on God and still be lost. No, tell him—

If all the sins that men have done
In thought or word or deed,
Since worlds were made or time begun,
Could meet on one poor head,
The blood of Jesus Christ alone
For all this guilt could well atone.

Oh, lay this to heart. May God's Spirit do it! "For everyone who calls on the name of the Lord will be saved."

How to Become Fishers of Men

No. 1906, Metropolitan Tabernacle, London, England

And Jesus said to them, "Follow me,
and I will make you fishers of men."
– Matthew 4:19

When Christ calls us by his grace, we ought not only to remember what we are but we ought also to *think of what he can make us*. It is "Follow me, and I will *make you*." We should repent of what we have been but rejoice in what we may be. It is not "Follow me because of what you already are" nor "Follow me because you may make something of yourselves" but "Follow me because of what I will make you."

I might truly say of each one of us, as soon as we are converted, "It does not yet appear what we shall be." It did not seem a likely thing that lowly fishermen would develop into apostles, that men so handy with the net would be quite as much at home in preaching sermons and in instructing converts! One would have said, "How can these things be? You cannot make founders of churches out of peasants of Galilee!" That is exactly what Christ did, and when we are brought low in the sight of God by a sense of our own unworthiness, we may feel encouraged to follow Jesus because of what he can make us.

What did the woman of a sorrowful spirit say when she lifted up her song? "He raises up the poor from the dust; he lifts the needy from the ash heap to make them sit with princes." We cannot tell what God may make of us in the new creation since it would have been quite impossible to have foretold what he made of chaos in the old creation. Who could have imagined all the beautiful things that came forth from darkness and disorder by that one fiat, "Let there be light"? And who can tell what lovely displays of everything divinely fair may yet appear in a man's formerly dark life when God's grace has said to him, "Let there be light"? O you who see in yourselves at present nothing that is desirable, come and follow Christ for the sake of what he can make out of you! Do you not hear his sweet voice calling to you and saying, "Follow me, and I will make you fishers of men"?

Note, next, that *we are not all made that we will be*, nor all that we ought to *desire* to be, when we are, ourselves, fished for and caught. This is what the grace of God does for us at first, but it is not all. We are like the fishes, making sin to be our element, and the good Lord comes, and with the gospel net, takes us and delivers us from the life and love of sin. But he has not worked for us all that he can do nor all that we should wish him to do when he has done this, for it is another and a higher miracle to make us, who were fish, to become fishers! To make the saved into saviors—to make the convert into a converter—the receiver of the gospel into an imparter of that same gospel to other people.

I think I may say to every person whom I am addressing—if you are saved, the work is but half done until you are employed to bring others to Christ! You are as yet but half formed in the image of your Lord. You have not attained to the full development of the Christ-life in you unless you have commenced, in some feeble way, to tell others of the grace of God—and I trust that you will find no rest for the soles of your feet till you have been the means of leading many to that blessed Savior, who is your confidence and your hope!

His word is "Follow me," not merely that you may be saved, nor even that you may be sanctified, but "Follow me, and I will make you fishers of men." Be following Christ with that intent and aim—and fear that you are not perfectly following him unless, in some degree, he is making use of you to be fishers of men. The fact is that every one of us must take to the business of a man-catcher. If Christ has caught us, we must catch others. If we have been apprehended by him, we must be his constables, to apprehend rebels for him! Let us ask him to give us grace to go fishing and so to cast our nets that we may take a great multitude of fish! Oh, that the Holy Spirit may raise up from among us some master fishermen who will sail their boats in many a sea and surround great shoals of fish!

My teaching at this time will be very simple, but I hope it will be eminently practical, for my longing is that not one of you who love the Lord may be backward in *serving* him. What does the Song of Solomon say concerning certain sheep that come up from the washing? It says, "Everyone bears twins, and none is barren among them." May that be so with all the members of this church and all the Christian people who hear or read this sermon!

The fact is the day is very dark. The heavens are lowering with heavy thunderclouds. Men little dream of what tempests may soon shake this city and the whole social fabric of this land—even to a general breaking up of society! So dark may the night become that the stars may seem to fall like blighted fruit from the trees. The times are evil! Now, if never before, every glowworm must show its spark. You with the tiniest farthing candle must take it from under the bushel and set it on a candlestick! There is need of you all! Lot was a poor creature. He was a very, very wretched kind of believer, but still, he might have been a great blessing to Sodom had he but pleaded for it as he should have done.

And poor, poor Christians, as I fear many are, one begins to value every truly converted soul in these evil days and to pray that each one may glorify the Lord. I pray that every righteous man, vexed as he is with the conversation of the wicked, may be more importunate in prayer than he has ever been, return to his God and get more spiritual life that he may be a blessing to the perishing people around him. I address you, therefore, at this time, first of all upon this thought. Oh, that the Spirit of God may make each one of you feel his personal responsibility!

Here is for believers in Christ, in order to their usefulness, something for them to do: "Follow me." But, secondly, here is something to be done by their great Lord and Master—"Follow me, and *I* will make you fishers of men!" You will not grow into fishermen by yourselves, but this is what Jesus will do for you if you will but follow him. And then, lastly, here is a good illustration, used according to our great Master's custom, for scarcely without a parable did he speak to the people. He presents us with an illustration of what Christian men should be—fishers of men. We may get some useful hints out of it, and I pray the Holy Spirit to bless them to us.

Something for You to Do

I will take it for granted that every believer here wants to be useful. If he does not, I take leave to question whether he can be a true believer in Christ. Well, then, if you really want to be useful, here is something for you to do—"Follow me, and I will make you fishers of men."

What is the way to become an efficient preacher? "Young man," says one, "go to college." "Young man," says Christ, "*follow me*, and I will make you a fisher of men."

How is a person to be useful? "Attend a training class," says one. Quite right, but there is a surer answer than that—follow Jesus, and he will make you fishers of men. The great training school for Christian workers has Christ at its head—not only as a Tutor but as a Leader. We are not only to learn of him in study but to follow him in action. "Follow me, and I will make you fishers of men."

The direction is very distinct and plain—and I believe that it is exclusive so that no man can become a fisherman by any other process. This process may appear to be very simple, but assuredly it is most efficient. The Lord Jesus Christ, who knew all about fishing for men, was himself the dictator of the rule, "Follow me, if you want to be fishers of men. If you would be useful, keep in my tracks."

I understand this, first, in this sense—*be separate unto Christ.* These men were to leave their pursuits. They were to leave their companions. They were, in fact, to quit the world so that their one business might be, in their Master's name, to be fishers of men. We are not all called to leave our daily business or to quit our families. That might be rather running away from the fishery than working at it in God's name. But we are called most distinctly to come out from among the ungodly, to be separate and not to touch the unclean thing! We cannot be fishers of men if we remain among men in the same element with them.

Fish will not be fishers! The sinner will not convert the sinner. The ungodly man will not convert the ungodly man, and what is more to the point, the worldly Christian will not convert the world! If you are of the world, no doubt the world will love its own, but you cannot save the world. If you are dark and belong to the kingdom of darkness, you cannot remove the darkness. If you march with the armies of the wicked one, you cannot defeat them!

I believe that one reason why the church of God, at this present moment, has so little influence over the world is because the world has so much influence over the church! Nowadays we hear Nonconformists pleading that they may do this, and they do that—things that their Puritan forefathers would rather have died at the stake than have tolerated! They plead that they may live like the ungodly, and my sad answer to them, when they crave for this liberty, is "Do it if you dare! It may not do you much hurt, for you are so bad already. Your cravings show how rotten your hearts are. If you have a hungering after such dog's meat, go, dogs, and eat the garbage! Worldly amusements are fit food for mere pretenders and hypocrites. If you were God's children, you would loathe the very *thought* of the world's evil joys, and your question would not be 'How far may we be like the world?' but your one cry would be 'How far can we get

away from the world? How much can we come out from it?'"
Your temptation would be rather to become sternly severe and
ultra-Puritanical in your separation from sin, in such a time as
this, than to ask, "How can I make myself like other men and act
as they do?"

Brothers, the use of the church in the world is that it should
be like salt in the midst of putrefaction—but if the salt has lost its
savor, what is the good of it? If it were possible for salt to putrefy,
it could but be an increase and a heightening of the general
putridity. The worst day the world ever saw was when the sons
of God were joined with the daughters of men. Then came the
flood—for the only barrier against a flood of vengeance on this
world is the separation of the saint from the sinner!

Your duty as a Christian is to stand fast in your own place
and stand out for God, hating even the garment spotted by the
flesh! Yours must be a resolve, like one of old, that, let others do
as they will, as for you and your house, you will serve the Lord!

Come, children of God, you *must* stand out with your Lord
outside the camp! Jesus calls to you, today, and says, "Follow
me." Was Jesus found at the theater? Did he frequent the sports
of the racecourse? Was Jesus seen, do you think, in any of the
amusements of the Herodian court? Not he! He was "holy,
harmless, undefiled and separate from sinners." In one sense,
no one mixed with sinners so completely as he did, when, like
a physician, he went among them healing his patients. But in
another sense, there was a gulf fixed between the men of the
world and the Savior that he never crossed and which they
could not cross to defile him.

The first lesson the church must learn is this: follow Jesus
into the separated state, and he will make you fishers of men.
Unless you take up your cross and protest against an ungodly
world, you cannot hope that the holy Jesus will make you fishers
of men.

A second meaning of our text is very obviously this: *abide
with Christ*, and then you will be made fishers of men. These
disciples whom Christ called were to come and live with him.

They were to be associated with him every day. They were to hear him publicly teach the everlasting gospel.

In addition, they were to receive choice explanations in private of the Word that he had spoken. They were to be his servants and his familiar friends. They were to see his miracles and hear his prayers, and better still, they were to be with him and become one with him in his holy labor. It was given to them to sit at the table with him and even to have their feet washed by him! Many of them fulfilled that Word of God, "Where you dwell, I will dwell"—they were with him in his afflictions and persecutions. They witnessed his secret agonies. They saw his many tears. They marked the passion and the compassion of his soul and thus, after their measure, they caught his spirit—and so they learned to be fishers of men.

At Jesus's feet we must learn the art and mystery of soul-winning! To live with Christ is the best education for usefulness. It is a great blessing to any man to be associated with a Christian minister whose heart is on fire. The best training for a young man is that which the Vaudois pastors were known to give when each old man had a young man with him who walked with him whenever he went up the mountainside to preach. He lived in the house with him and marked his prayers and saw his daily piety. This was a fine instruction, was it not? But it does not compare with that of the apostles who lived with Jesus and were his daily companions! Matchless was the training of the twelve.

No wonder that they became what they were with such a heavenly tutor to saturate them with his own Spirit! And now, today, his bodily presence is not among us, but his spiritual power is, perhaps, more fully known to us than it was to those apostles in those two or three years of the Lord's corporeal presence.

There are some of us to whom he is intimately near. We know more about him than we do about our dearest earthly friend. We have never been quite able to read our friend's heart in all its twists and turns, but we know the heart of the Well-Beloved! We have placed our head on his bosom and have enjoyed fellowship with him, such as we could not have with any of our own kith and kin! This is the surest method of learning how to do good. Live with Jesus, follow Jesus, and he will make you fishers of men!

Watch how he does the work and so learn how to do it yourself. A Christian man should be a bound apprentice to Jesus to learn the trade of a savior! We can never save men by offering a redemption, for we have none to present, but we can learn how to save men by warning them to flee from the wrath to come and setting before them the one great effectual Remedy! Watch how Jesus saves, and you will learn how the thing is done—there is no learning it anyway else! Live in fellowship with Christ, and there will be about you an air and a manner as of one who has been made in heart and mind, apt to teach, and wise to win souls.

A third meaning, however, must be given to this "Follow me," and it is this, "*Obey me*, and then you shall know what to do to save men." We must not talk about our fellowship with Christ or our being separated from the world unto him unless we make him our Master and Lord in everything.

Some public teachers are not true in all points to their convictions, so how can *they* look for a blessing? A Christian man, anxious to be useful, ought to be very particular as to every point of obedience to his Master. I have no doubt whatsoever that God blesses our churches even when they are very faulty, for his mercy endures forever. When there is a measure of error in the teaching and a measure of mistake in the practice, God may still vouchsafe to use the ministry, for he is very gracious. But a large measure of blessing must necessarily be withheld from all teaching that is knowingly or glaringly faulty.

God can set his seal upon the truth that is in it, but he *cannot* set his seal upon the *error* that is in it! Out of mistakes about Christian ordinances and other things, especially errors in heart and spirit, there may come evils that we never looked for. Such evils may even now be telling upon the present age and may work worse mischief on future generations. If we desire, as fishers of men, to be largely used of God, we must copy our Lord Jesus in everything and obey him in *every point*.

Failure in obedience may lead to failure in success. Each one of us, if he would wish to see his child saved or his Sunday school class blessed or his congregation converted, must take care that, bearing the vessels of the Lord, he is, himself, clean. Anything we do that grieves the Spirit of God must take away from us some part of our power for good.

The Lord is very gracious and full of pity, but he is a jealous God. He is sometimes sternly jealous toward his people who are living in neglects of known duty or in associations that are not clean in his sight. He will wither their work, weaken their strength, and humble them until, at last, they say, "My Lord, I will take your way after all. I will do what you bid me to do, for otherwise you will not accept me." The Lord said to his disciples, "Go into all the world and preach the gospel to every creature: he that believes and is baptized shall be saved." And he promised them that signs would follow, and so they did follow them, and so they will.

And so, we must get back to apostolic practice and to apostolic teaching—we must lay aside the commandments of men and the whims of our own brains and we must do *what* Christ tells us, *as* Christ tells us, and *because* Christ tells us! Definitely and distinctly, we must take the place of *servants*—and if we will not do that, we cannot expect our Lord to work *with* us or *by* us. Let us be determined that, as true as the needle is to the pole, so true will we be, as far as our light goes, to the command of our Lord and Master. Jesus says, "Follow me, and I will make you fishers of men." By this teaching he seems to say, "Go beyond me, or fall behind me, and you may cast the net, but it shall be night with you, and that night you shall take nothing. When you shall do as I bid you, you shall cast your net on the right side of the ship, and you shall find."

Again, I think there is a great lesson in my text to those who preach their own thoughts instead of preaching the thoughts of Christ. These disciples were to follow Christ that they might listen to him, hear what he had to say, drink in his teaching, and then *go and teach what he had taught them*. Their Lord says,

"What I tell you in the dark, say in the light, and what you hear whispered, proclaim on the housetops." If they will be faithful reporters of Christ's message, he will make them "fishers of men."

But you know the boastful method, nowadays, is this: "I am not going to preach this old, old gospel, this musty Puritan doctrine! I will sit down in my study, burn the midnight oil, and invent a new theory—then I will come out with my brand-new thought and blaze away with it!" Many are not following Christ but following themselves—and of them the Lord may well say, "You shall see whose word shall stand, mine or theirs."

Others are wickedly prudent and judge that certain truths that are evidently God's Word had better be kept back. You must not be rough but must prophesy smooth things! To talk about the punishment of sin, to speak of eternal punishment, why, these are unfashionable doctrines! It may be that they are taught in the Word of God, but they do not suit the genius of the age. We must pare them down. Brothers in Christ, I will have no share in this! Will you? O my Soul, come not into their secret! Certain things not taught in the Bible, our enlightened age has discovered. Evolution may be clean contrary to the teaching of Genesis, but that does not matter! We are not going to be believers of Scripture but original thinkers. This is the boastful ambition of the period! Mark you, in proportion as the modern theology is preached, the vice of this generation increases!

To a great degree, I attribute the looseness of the age to the laxity of the doctrine preached by its teachers. From the pulpit they have taught the people that sin is a trifle. From the pulpit these traitors to God and to his Christ have taught the people that there is no hell to be feared! A little, little hell, perhaps, there may be—but just punishment for sin is made nothing of! The precious atoning sacrifice of Christ has been derided and misrepresented by those who were pledged to preach it! They have given the people the name of the gospel, but the gospel itself has evaporated in their hands. From hundreds of pulpits the gospel is as clean gone as the dodo from its old haunts—and still the preachers take the position and name of Christ's ministers!

Well, and what comes of it? Why, their congregations grow thinner and thinner—and so it must be. Jesus says, "Follow me, I will make you fishers of men," but if you go in your own way, with your own net, you will make nothing of it, and the Lord promises you no help in it. The Lord's directions make himself our leader and example! It is "Follow me, follow me! Preach my gospel. Preach what I preached! Teach what I taught, and keep to that!" With that blessed servility that becomes one whose ambition it is to be a copyist and never to be an original, copy Christ, even in jots and tittles! Do this, and he will make you fishers of men! But if you do *not* do this, you will fish in vain.

I close this head of discourse by saying that we shall not be fishers of men unless we follow Christ in one other respect, and that is, by endeavoring in all points, to *imitate his holiness*. Holiness is the most real power that can be possessed by men or women.

We may preach orthodoxy, but we must also *live* orthodoxy. God forbid that we should preach anything else, but it will be all in vain unless there is a life at the back of the testimony. An unholy preacher may even render the truth of God contemptible! In proportion, as any of us draw back from a living and zealous sanctification, we will draw back from the place of power. Our power lies in this word, "Follow me." Be Jesus-like!

In all things, endeavor to think, speak, and act as Jesus did—and he will make you fishers of men. This will require self-denial. We must daily take up the cross. This may require willingness to give up our reputation—readiness to be called fools, idiots, and the like, as men are apt to call those who are keeping close to their Master. There must be the cheerful resigning of *everything* that looks like honor and personal glory in order that we may be wholly Christ's and glorify his name.

We must live his life and be ready to die his death, if need be. O brothers and sisters, if we do this and follow Jesus, putting our feet into the footprints of his pierced feet, he will make us fishers of men! If it should so please him that we should even die without having gathered many souls to the cross, we shall speak from our graves! In some way or other, the Lord will make a holy life to be an influential life! It is not possible that a life that can be described as a following of Christ should be an unsuccessful one in the sight of the Most High. "Follow me," and there is an "I will" such as God can never draw back from—"Follow me, and I *will* make you fishers of men."

Thus, much on the first point. There is something for us to do—we are graciously called to follow Jesus. Holy Spirit, lead us to do it!

Something for the Lord to Do

But secondly, and briefly, there is *something for the Lord to do*. When his dear servants are following him, he says, "I will make you fishers of men," and be it never forgotten that it is he who makes us follow him, so that if the following of him is the step to being made a fisher of men, yet he gives this to us! This is all of his Spirit. I have talked about catching his spirit, abiding in him, obeying him, listening to him and copying him—but none of these things are we capable of apart from his working them all in us! "From me is your fruit found" is a text we must not, for a moment, forget! So, then, if we do follow him, it is he who makes us follow him, and so *he makes us fishers of men*.

But, further, if we follow Christ, he will make us fishers of men *by all our experience*. I am sure that the man who is really consecrated to bless others will be helped in this by all that he feels, especially by his afflictions. I often feel very grateful to God that I have undergone fearful depression of spirits. I know the borders of despair and the horrible brink of that gulf of darkness into which my feet have almost gone—but hundreds of times I have been able to give a helpful grip to brothers and sisters who have come into that same condition, which grip I could never have given if I had not known their deep despondency myself. So, I believe that the darkest and most dreadful experience of a child of God will help him to be a fisher of men if he will but follow Christ. Keep close to your Lord, and he will make every step a blessing to you.

If God, in providence, should make you rich, he will fit you to speak to those ignorant and wicked rich who so much abound in this city—and so often are the cause of its worst sin. And if the Lord is pleased to let you be very poor, you can go down and talk to those wicked and ignorant poor people who so often are the cause of sin in this city—and so greatly need the gospel. The winds of providence will take you where you can fish for men! The wheels of providence are full of eyes, and all those eyes will look this way to help us be winners of souls! You will often be surprised to find how God has been in a house you visit—before you get there, his hands have been at work in its chambers!

When you wish to speak to some particular individual, God's providence has been dealing with that individual to make him ready for just that Word of God you will say but which nobody else but you could say. Oh, follow Christ and you will find that he will, by every experience through which you are passing, make you fishers of men!

Further than that, if you will follow him, he will make you fishers of men *by distinct monitions in your own heart*. There are many monitions from God's Spirit not noticed by Christians when they are in a callous condition. But when the heart is right with God and living in communion with God, we feel a sacred sensitiveness so that we do not need the Lord to shout, but his faintest whisper is heard. No, he need not even whisper. "You shall guide me with your eyes." Oh, how many mulish Christians there are who must be held in with bit and bridle—and receive a cut of the whip every now and then! But the Christian who follows his Lord shall be tenderly guided.

I do not say that the Spirit of God will say to you, "Go and join yourself to this chariot," or that you will hear a word in your ears—but yet in your soul, as distinctly as the Spirit said to Philip, "Go and join yourself to this chariot," you shall hear the Lord's will! As soon as you see an individual, the thought shall cross your mind, "Go and speak to that person." Every opportunity of usefulness will be a call to you. If you are ready, the door will open before you, and you will hear a voice behind you saying, "This is the way; walk in it." If you have the grace to run in the right way, you will never be long without an intimation as to what the right way is! That right way will lead you to river or sea, where you can cast your net and be a fisher of men.

Then, too, I believe that the Lord meant by this that *he would give his followers the Holy Spirit*. They were to follow him and then, when they had seen him ascend into the Holy Place of the Most High, they were to tarry at Jerusalem for a little while, and the Spirit would come upon them and clothe them with a mysterious power. This word was spoken to Peter and Andrew, and you know how it was fulfilled to Peter! What a host of fish he brought to land the first time he cast the net in the power of the Holy Spirit! "Follow me, and I will make you fishers of men."

Brethren, we have no conception of what God could do by this company of believers gathered in the Tabernacle tonight. If now we were to be filled with the Holy Spirit, there are enough of us to evangelize London! There are enough here to be the means of the salvation of the world! God saves not by many nor by few. Let us seek a benediction, and if we seek it, let us hear this directing voice: "Follow me, and I will make you fishers of men."

You men and women who sit before me, you are by the shore of a great sea of human life swarming with the souls of men! You live amid millions—and if you will follow Jesus and be faithful to him and true to him and do what he bids you, he will make you fishers of men!

Do not ask, "Who will save this city?" The weakest will be strong enough! Gideon's barley cake will smite the tent and make it fall down! Samson, with the jawbone taken up from the earth, where it was lying bleaching in the sun, will smite the Philistines! Fear not, neither be dismayed! Let your responsibilities drive you closer to your Master. Let horror of prevailing sin make you look into his dear face who long ago wept over Jerusalem and now weeps over London. Clasp him, and never let go! By the strong and mighty impulses of the Divine life within you, quickened and brought to maturity by the Spirit of God, learn this lesson from your Lord's own mouth—"Follow me, and I will make you fishers of men."

You are not fit for it, but he will make you fit! You cannot do it by yourselves, but he will make you do it! You do not know how to spread nets and draw shoals of fish to shore, but he will teach you! Only follow him, and he will make you fishers of men!

I wish that I could somehow say this as with a voice of thunder, that the whole church of God might hear it. I wish I could write it in stars across the sky, "Jesus says, 'Follow me, and I will make you fishers of men.'" If you forget the precept, the promise will never be yours. If you follow some other track or imitate some other leader, you will fish in vain. God grant us to believe fully that Jesus can do great things *in* us—and then do great things *by* us for the good of our fellows!

A Figure Full of Instruction

The last point you might work out in full, for yourselves, in your private meditations, with much profit. We have here a figure full of instruction. I will give you but two or three thoughts you can use. "I will make you *fishers of men*." You have been fishers of *fish*—if you follow me, I will make you fishers of *men*.

A fisher is a person who is *very dependent and needs to be trustful*. He cannot see the fish. One who fishes in the sea must go and cast in a net, as it were, at an uncertainty. Fishing is an act of faith. I have often seen, in the Mediterranean, men go with their boats and enclose acres of sea with vast nets, and yet, when they have drawn the net to shore, they have not had as much result as I could put in my hand! A few wretched silvery nothings have made up the whole take. Yet they have gone again and cast the great net several times a day, hopefully expecting something to come of it.

Nobody is so dependent on God as the minister of God! Oh, this fishing from the Tabernacle pulpit! What a work of faith! I cannot tell that a soul will be brought to God by it. I cannot judge whether my sermon will be suitable to the persons who are here, except that I do believe that God will guide me in the casting of the net! I expect *him* to work salvation, and I depend on him for it! I love this complete dependence, and if I could be offered a certain amount of preaching power by which I could save sinners, which should be entirely at my own disposal, I would beg the Lord not to let me have it, for it is far more delightful to be entirely dependent on him at all times!

It is good to be a fool when Christ is made wisdom unto you. It is a blessed thing to be weak if Christ becomes more fully your strength! Go to work, you who would be fishers of men, and yet feel your insufficiency. You that have no strength, attempt this Divine work! Your Master's strength will be seen when your own has all gone. A fisherman is a dependent person. He must look up for success every time he puts the net down, but still, he is a trustful person, and therefore, he casts in the net joyfully.

A fisherman who gets his living by it is *a diligent and persevering man*. The fishers are up at dawn. At daybreak our fishermen off the Dogger Bank are fishing, and they continue fishing till late in the afternoon. As long as hands can work, men will fish. May the Lord Jesus make us hardworking, persevering, unwearied fishers of men! "In the morning sow your seed, and at evening withhold not your hand, for you do not know which will prosper, this or that" (Eccl. 11:6).

The fisherman, in his own craft, is *intelligent and watchful*. It looks very easy, I dare say, to be a fisherman, but you would find that it was no child's play if you were to take a real try at it. There is an art in it, from the mending of the net, right on to the pulling it to shore. How diligent the fisherman is to prevent the fish leaping out of the net!

I heard a great noise one night in the sea, as if some huge drum were being beaten by a giant. I looked out, and I saw that the fishermen of Mentone were beating the water to drive the fish into the net or to keep them from leaping out when they had once encompassed them with it. Ah, yes, and you and I will often have to be watching the corners of the Gospel net lest sinners who are almost caught should make their escape. They are very crafty, these fish, and they use this craftiness in endeavoring to avoid salvation! We must always be at our business and exercise all our wits, and *more* than our wits, if we are to be successful fishers of men!

The fisherman is *a very laborious person*. It is not at all an easy calling. He does not sit in an armchair and catch fish. He has to go out in rough weather. If he who regards the clouds will not sow, I am sure that he who regards the clouds will never fish. If we never do any work for Christ except when we feel up to the mark, we will not do much. If we feel we will not pray because we cannot pray, we will never pray! And if we say, "I will not preach today because I do not feel that I could preach," we will never preach any preaching that is worth the preaching! We must always be at it until we wear ourselves out, throwing our whole soul into the work, for Christ's sake, in all weather.

The fisherman is *a daring man*. He tempts the boisterous sea. A little brine in his face does not hurt him. He has been wet through and through a thousand times—it is nothing to him. He never expected, when he became a deep-sea fisherman, that he was going to sleep in the lap of ease. So, the true minister of Christ who fishes for souls will never mind a little risk. He will be bound to do or say many a thing that is very unpopular—and some Christians may even judge his utterances to be too severe. He must do and say that which is for the good of souls. It is not his to entertain a question as to what others will think of his doctrine or of him—but in the name of the Almighty God he must feel "if the sea roars and the fullness thereof, still, at my Master's command, I will let down the net."

Now, in the last place, the man whom Christ makes a fisher of men *is successful*. "But," says one, "I have always heard that Christ's ministers are to be faithful but that they cannot be sure of being successful." Yes, I have heard that saying, and in one way I know it is true, but in another way I have my doubts about it. He that is faithful is, in God's way and in God's judgment, successful, more or less. For instance, here is a brother who says he is faithful. Of course, I must believe him, yet I never heard of a sinner being saved under him. Indeed, I would think that the safest place for a person to be in, if he did not want to be saved, would be under this gentleman's ministry because he does not preach anything that is likely to awaken, impress, or convict anybody! This brother is "faithful," so he says.

Well, if any person in the world said to you, "I am a fisherman, but I have never caught anything," you would wonder how he could be called a fisherman, wouldn't you? A farmer who never grew any wheat or any other crop—is he a farmer? When Jesus Christ says, "Follow me, and I will make you fishers of men," he means that you will really catch men, that you will really save some, for he who never did get any fish is not a fisherman!

He who never saved a sinner after years of work is not a minister of Christ. If the result of his life's work is zero, he made a mistake when he undertook it. Go with the fire of God in your hands and fling it among the stubble, and the stubble will burn. You can be sure of that! Go and scatter the good seed—it may not all fall in fruitful places, but some of it will. You can be sure of that! Do but shine, and some eyes or other will be lightened! You must—you *will*—succeed. But remember, this is the Lord's word—"Follow me, and I will make you fishers of men." Keep close to Jesus and do as Jesus did, in his Holy Spirit, and he will make you fishers of men.

Perhaps I speak to an attentive heart who is not converted at all. Friend, I have the same thing to say to you. You, also, may follow Christ, and then he can use you, even you. I do not know if he hasn't brought you to this place that you may be saved and that in later years he may make you speak for his name and glory. Remember how he called Saul of Tarsus and made him the apostle of the Gentiles? Reclaimed poachers make the best gamekeepers, and saved sinners make the most able preachers!

Oh, that you would run away from your old master, tonight, without giving him a minute's notice—for if you give him any notice, he will hold you. Hasten to Jesus and say, "Here is a poor runaway slave! My Lord, I bear the fetters still upon my wrists. Will you set me free and make me your own?" Remember, it is written, "Whoever comes to me I will never cast out" (John 6:37). Never has a runaway slave came to Christ in the middle of the night without his taking him in—and he never gave one up to his old master! If Jesus makes you free, you shall be free, indeed! Flee away to Jesus, then, right now! May his good Spirit help you, and he will, by-and-by, make you a winner of others to his praise! God bless you. Amen.

The Dying Thief in a New Light

No. 1881, Metropolitan Tabernacle, London, England
August 23, 1885

But the other rebuked him, saying, "Do you not fear God, since
you are under the same sentence of condemnation? And
we indeed justly, for we are receiving the due reward of our
deeds; but this man has done nothing wrong." And he said,
"Jesus, remember me when you come into your kingdom."
– Luke 23:40–42

Too many people, whenever they hear of the conversion of the
dying thief, remember that he was saved at the very point of
death, and they dwell upon that fact and that alone. He has always been quoted as a case of salvation at the eleventh hour; and
so, indeed, he is. In his case it is proven that as long as a man can
repent, he can obtain forgiveness. The cross of Christ avails even
for a man hanging on a scaffold and drawing near to his last hour.
He who is mighty to save was mighty even during his own death
to pluck others from the grasp of the destroyer, though they were
in the act of expiring.

But that is not everything the story teaches us, and it is
always a pity to look exclusively on one point and thus miss
everything else—perhaps miss that which is more important. So

often has this been the case that it has produced a sort of revulsion of feeling in certain minds so that they have been driven in a wrong direction by their wish to protest against what they think to be a common error. I read the other day that this story of the dying thief ought not to be taken as an encouragement to death-bed repentance.

Brethren, if the author meant—and I do not think he did mean—that this ought never to be so used as to lead people to postpone repentance to a dying bed, he spoke correctly. No Christian man could or would use it so injuriously; he must be hopelessly bad who would draw from God's longsuffering an argument for continuing in sin.

I trust, however, that the narrative is not often so used, even by the worst of men, and I feel sure that it will not be so used by any one of you. It cannot be properly turned to such a purpose. It might be used as an encouragement to steal just as much as to the delay of repentance. I might say, "I may be a thief because this thief was saved," just as rationally as I might say, "I may put off repentance because this thief was saved when he was about to die." The fact is, there is nothing so good, but men can pervert it into evil, if they have evil hearts. The justice of God is made a motive for despair, and his mercy an argument for sin.

Wicked men will drown themselves in the rivers of truth as readily as in the pools of error. He who has a mind to destroy himself can choke his soul with the Bread of Life or dash himself in pieces against the Rock of Ages. There is no doctrine of the grace of God so gracious that graceless men may not turn it into licentiousness.

I venture, however, to say that if I stood by the bedside of a dying man tonight and I found him anxious about his soul but fearful that Christ could not save him because repentance had been put off so late, I should certainly quote the dying thief to him, and I should do it with good conscience and without hesitation. I should tell him that, though he was as near to dying as the thief upon the cross was, yet if he repented of his sin and turned his face to Christ believingly, he would find eternal life. I should do this with all my heart, rejoicing that I had such a story to tell to one at the gates of eternity. I do not think I should be censured by the Holy Spirit for thus using a narrative that he has himself recorded—recorded with the foresight that it would be so used. I should feel, at any rate, in my own heart, a sweet conviction that I had treated the subject as I ought to have treated it, and as it was intended to be used for men in extremis whose hearts are turning toward the living God.

Oh, yes, poor soul, whatever your age or whatever the period of life to which you have come, you may now find eternal life by faith in Christ!

> The dying thief rejoiced to see
> that fountain in his day;
> And there may you, though vile as he,
> Wash all your sins away.

Many good people think they ought to guard the gospel, but it is never so safe as when it stands out in its own naked majesty. It wants no covering from us. When we protect it with provisos and guard it with exceptions and qualify it with observations, it is like David in Saul's armor: hampered and hindered.

Leave the gospel alone, and it will save. I have heard it said that few are ever converted in old age. This is thought to be a statement that will prove exceedingly arousing and impressive for the young. It certainly wears that appearance at least. On the other hand, it is a very discouraging statement to the old. I demur the frequent repetition of such statements, for I do not find their counterpart in the teaching of our Lord and his apostles. Assuredly our Lord spoke of some who entered the vineyard at the eleventh hour of the day. And among his miracles he not only saved those who were dying but even raised the dead. Nothing can be concluded from the words of the Lord Jesus against the salvation of men at any hour or age. I tell you that any may be saved by faith in Christ Jesus, no matter their age.

The same promise is to every one of you: "Today if ye will hear his voice, harden not your hearts," and whether you are in the earliest stage of life or are within a few hours of eternity, if you fly for refuge to the hope set before you in the gospel, you will be saved. The gospel I preach excludes none on the ground either of age or character. Whoever you may be, "believe on the Lord Jesus Christ, and you shall be saved." This is the message we deliver to you.

If we address to you the longer form of the gospel, "He that believeth and is baptized shall be saved," this is true of every living man, be his age whatever it may. I am not afraid that this story of the dying and repenting thief, who went straight from the cross to the crown, will be used by you amiss, but if you are wicked enough so to use it, I cannot help it. It will only fulfill that solemn Scripture that says that the gospel is a savor of death unto death to some, even that very gospel that is a savor of life unto life to others (2 Cor. 2:16).

But I do not think, dear friends, that the only thing unique about the thief is the lateness of his repentance. So far from being the only point of interest, it is not even the chief point. To some minds, at any rate, other points will be even more remarkable. I want to show you very briefly that there was a uniqueness in his case as to the means of his conversion; secondly, a uniqueness in his faith; thirdly, a uniqueness in the result of his faith; and, fourthly, a uniqueness in the promise gained by his faith.

The Uniqueness of the Thief's Conversion

First, then, we should notice the uniqueness of the means by which the thief was converted. How do you think it was? Well, we do not know. We cannot tell. It seems to me that the man was an unconverted, impenitent thief when they nailed him to the cross, because one of the evangelists says, "And the robbers who were crucified with him also reviled him in the same way" (Matt. 27:44).

I know this may have been a general statement and that it is reconcilable with its having been done by one thief only, according to the methods commonly used by critics. But I am not enamored of critics even when they are friendly. I have such respect for revelation that I never in my own mind permit the idea of discrepancies and mistakes, and when the Evangelist says "they," I believe he meant "they," and that both these thieves did at their first crucifixion rail at the Christ with whom they were crucified. It would appear that by some means or other, this thief must have been converted while he was on the cross.

Assuredly, nobody preached a sermon to him, no evangelistic address was delivered at the foot of his cross, and no meeting was held for special prayer on his account. He does not even seem to have had an instruction, an invitation, or an expostulation addressed to him. And yet this man became a sincere and accepted believer in the Lord Jesus Christ.

Dwell upon this fact, if you please, and note its practical bearing on the cases of many around us. There are many among my hearers who have been instructed from their childhood, who have been admonished and warned and entreated and invited, and yet they have not come to Christ, while this man, without any of these advantages, nevertheless believed in the Lord Jesus Christ and found eternal life. O you who have lived under the sound of the gospel from your childhood, the thief does not comfort you—he accuses you! What are you doing to abide so long in unbelief? Will you never believe the testimony of divine love? What more must I say to you? What more can anyone say to you?

What do you think must have converted this poor thief? It strikes me that it may have been, it *must* have been, the sight of our great Lord and Savior. There was, to begin with, our Savior's wonderful behavior on the road to the cross. Perhaps the robber had mixed up with all sorts of society, but he had never seen a man like this. Never had a cross been carried by a cross-bearer of his look and fashion. The robber wondered who this meek and majestic personage could be. He heard the women weep, and he wondered in himself whether anybody would ever weep for him. He thought that this must be some very singular person that the people should stand about him with tears in their eyes. When he heard that mysterious sufferer say so solemnly, "Daughters of Jerusalem, weep not for me, but for your children" (Luke 23:28), he must have been struck with wonder. When he came to think, in his death pangs, of the singular look of pity Jesus cast on the women and of the self-forgetfulness that gleamed from his eyes, he was smitten with a strange relenting. It was as if an angel had crossed his path and opened his eyes to a new world and to a new form of humanity, the like of which he had never seen before.

He and his companion were coarse, rough fellows; this was a delicately formed and fashioned being, of superior order to himself, yes, and of superior order to any other of the sons of men. Who could he be? What must he be? Though he could see that he suffered and fainted as he went along, he marked that there was no word of complaining, no note of execration, in return for the reviling cast upon him. His eyes looked with love on those who glared on him with hate. Surely that march along the Via Dolorosa was the first part of the sermon God preached to that bad man's heart. It was preached to many others who did not regard its teaching, but upon this man, by God's special grace, it had a softening effect when he came to think over it and consider it. Was it not a likely and convincing means of grace?

When he saw the Savior surrounded by the Roman soldiery—saw the executioners bring forth the hammers and the nails and lay him down on his back and drive the nails into his hands and feet—this crucified criminal was startled and astonished as he heard him say, "Father, forgive them; for they know not what they do" (Luke 23:34). He himself, probably, had met his executioners with a curse. But he heard this man breathe a prayer to the great Father, and as a Jew, as he probably was, he understood what was meant by such a prayer. But it did astound him to hear Jesus pray for his murderers. That was a petition the like of which he had never heard nor even dreamed of. From whose lips could it come but from the lips of a divine being? Such a loving, forgiving, Godlike prayer proved him to be the Messiah. Who else had ever prayed so? Certainly not David and the kings of Israel, who, on the contrary, in all honesty and heartiness imprecated the wrath of God upon their enemies. Elijah himself would not have prayed in that fashion; rather, would he have called fire from heaven on the centurion and his company. It was a new, strange sound to him. I do not suppose he appreciated it to the full, but I can well believe it deeply impressed him and made him feel that his fellow-sufferer was a being about whom there was an exceeding mystery of goodness.

And when the cross was lifted up, that thief, hanging up on his own cross, looked around, and I suppose he could see that inscription written in three languages: "Jesus of Nazareth, the King of the Jews." If so, that writing was his little Bible, his New Testament, and he interpreted it by what he knew of the Old Testament. Putting this and that together—that strange person, incarnate loveliness, all patience and all majesty, that strange prayer, and now this singular inscription, surely he who knew the Old Testament, as I have no doubt he did, would say to himself, "Is this he? Is this truly the King of the Jews? This is he who wrought miracles and raised the dead and said he was the Son of God. Is it all true, and is he really our Messiah?"

Then he would remember the words of the prophet Isaiah, "He was despised and rejected by men, a man of sorrows and acquainted with grief. . . . Surely, he has borne our griefs and carried our sorrows" (Isa. 53:3–4). "Why," he would say to himself, "I never understood that passage in the prophet Isaiah before, but it must point to him. The chastisement of our peace is upon him. Can this be he who cried in the Psalms—'They have pierced my hands and feet' (Ps. 22:16)?" As he looked at him again, he felt in his soul, "It must be he? Could there be another so like to him?" He felt conviction creeping over his spirit. Then he looked again, and he marked how all men down below rejected and despised and hissed at him and hooted him, and all this would make the case the clearer:

All who see me mock me;
they make mouths at me; they wag their heads,
"He trusts in the Lord; let him deliver him;
let him rescue him, for he delights in him!"

Perhaps this dying thief read the gospel out of the lips of Christ's enemies. They said, "He saved others." "Ah," he thought, "did he save others? Why should he not save me?" What a grand bit of gospel that was for the dying thief: "He saved others!" I think I could swim to heaven on that plank, "He saved others," because if he saved others, he can surely save me.

Thus, the very things the enemies disdainfully threw at Christ would be gospel to this poor dying man. When it has been my misery to read any of the wretched prints that are sent us out of scorn, in which our Lord is held up to ridicule, I have thought, "Why, perhaps those who read these loathsome blasphemies may, nevertheless, learn the gospel from them!" You may pick a jewel from a dunghill and find its radiance undiminished, and you may gather the gospel from a blasphemous mouth and it will be nonetheless the gospel of salvation. Perhaps this man learned the gospel from those who jested at our dying Lord, and so, the servants of the devil were unconsciously made to be the servants of Christ.

But after all, surely that which won him most must have been to look at Jesus again, as he was hanging upon the cruel tree. Possibly nothing about the physical person of Christ would be attractive to him, for his visage was more marred than that of any man and his form more than the sons of men. But yet there must have been in that blessed face a singular charm. Was it not the very image of perfection?

As I conceive the face of Christ, it was very different from anything any painter has yet been able to place upon his canvas. It was all goodness and kindness and unselfishness, and yet it was a royal face. It was a face of superlative justice and unrivalled tenderness. Righteousness and uprightness sat upon his brow, but infinite pity and goodwill to men had also there taken up their abode. It was a face that would have struck you at once as one by itself, never to be forgotten, never to be fully understood. It was all sorrow yet all love, all meekness yet all resolution, all wisdom yet all simplicity, the face of a child or an angel and yet peculiarly the face of a man.

Majesty and misery, suffering and sacredness, were therein strangely combined. He was evidently the Lamb of God and the

Son of Man. As the robber looked, he believed. Is it not singular, the very sight of the Master won him? The sight of the Lord in agony and shame and death! Scarcely a word—certainly, no sermon, no attending worship on the Sabbath, no reading of gracious books, no appeal from mother or teacher or friend. But the sight of Jesus won him. I put it down as a very singular thing, a thing for you and for me to recollect and dwell upon with quite as much vividness as we do upon the lateness of this robber's conversion.

Oh, that God of his mercy might convert everybody in this Tabernacle! Oh, that I could have a share in it by the preaching of the Word! But I will be equally happy if you get to heaven anyhow; aye, if the Lord should take you there without outward ministries, leading you to Jesus by some simple method such as he adopted with this thief. If you do but get there, he will have the glory of it, and his poor servant will be overjoyed! Oh, that you would now look to Jesus and live! Before your eyes he is set forth, evidently crucified among you. Look to him and be saved, even at this hour.

The Uniqueness of This Man's Faith

But now I want you to think with me a little on the uniqueness of this man's faith. I think it was a very singular faith this man exerted toward our Lord Jesus Christ. I greatly question whether the equal and the parallel of the dying thief's faith will be readily found outside the Scriptures, or even in the Scriptures.

Observe, that this man believed in Christ when he literally saw him dying the death of a felon, under circumstances of the greatest personal shame. You have never realized what it was to be crucified. None of you could do that, for the sight has never been seen in our day in England. There is not a man or woman here who has ever realized in their own mind the actual death of Christ. It stands beyond us.

This man saw it with his own eyes, and for him to call him "Lord," who was hanging on a tree, was no small triumph of faith. For him to ask Jesus to remember him when he came into his kingdom, though he saw that Jesus bleeding his life away and hounded to the death, was a splendid act of reliance. For him to commit his everlasting destiny into the hands of One who was, to all appearance, unable even to preserve his own life, was a noble achievement of faith. I say that this dying thief leads the van in the matter of faith, for what he saw of the circumstances of the Savior was calculated to contradict rather than help his confidence. What he saw was to his hindrance rather than to his help, for he saw our Lord in the very extremity of agony and death, and yet he believed in him as the King shortly to come into his kingdom.

Recollect, too, that at that moment when the thief believed in Christ, all the disciples had forsaken him and fled. John might be lingering at a little distance, and holy women may have stood farther off, but no one was present bravely to champion the dying Christ. Judas had sold him, Peter had denied him, and the rest had forsaken him, and it was then that the dying thief called him "Lord," and said, "Remember me when you come into your kingdom."

I call that splendid faith. Why, some of you do not believe, though you are surrounded with Christian friends—though you are urged on by the testimony of those whom you regard with love. But this man, all alone, comes out, and calls Jesus his Lord! No one else was confessing Christ at that moment: no revival was around him with enthusiastic crowds. He was all by himself as a confessor of his Lord. After our Lord was nailed to the tree, the first to bear witness for him was this thief.

The centurion bore witness afterward, when our Lord expired. But this thief was a lone confessor, holding on to Christ when nobody would say amen to what he said. Even his fellow-thief was mocking at the crucified Savior, so that this man shone as a lone star in the midnight darkness. O sirs, dare you be Daniels? Dare you stand alone? Would you dare to stand out amid a ribald crew and say, "Jesus is my King; I only ask him to remember me when he comes into his kingdom"? Would you be likely to avow such a faith when priests and scribes, princes and people, were all mocking the Christ and deriding him? Brethren, the dying robber exhibited marvelous faith, and I beg you to think of this next time you speak of him.

And it seems to me that another point adds splendor to that faith—namely, that he himself was in extreme torture. Remember, he was crucified. It was a crucified man trusting in a crucified Christ. Oh, when our frame is racked with torture, when the tenderest nerves are pained, when our body is hung up to die, by what great length of torment we know not, then to forget the present and live in the future is a grand achievement of faith! While dying, to turn one's eye to Another dying at your side, and trust your soul with him, is very marvelous faith. Blessed thief, because they put you down at the bottom, as one of the least of saints, I think I must bid you come up higher and take one of the uppermost seats among those who by faith have glorified the Christ of God!

Why, see, dear friends, once more, the uniqueness of this man's faith was that he saw so much, though his eyes had been opened for so short a time! He saw the future world. He was not a believer in annihilation or in the possibility of a man's not being immortal. He evidently expected to be in another world and to be in existence when the dying Lord should come into his kingdom. He believed all that, and it is more than some do nowadays. He also believed that Jesus would have a kingdom, a kingdom after he was dead, a kingdom though he was crucified. He believed that he was winning for himself a kingdom by those nailed hands and pierced feet.

This was intelligent faith, was it not? He believed that Jesus would have a kingdom in which others would share, and therefore he aspired to have his portion in it. But yet he had fit views of himself, and therefore he did not say, "Lord, let me sit at your right hand," or, "Let me share of the dainties of your palace," but he said only, "Remember me. Think of me. Cast an eye my way. Think of your poor dying comrade on the cross at your right hand. Lord, remember me. Remember me." I see deep humility in the prayer and yet a sweet, joyous, confident exaltation of the Christ at the time when the Christ was in his deepest humiliation.

O dear sirs, if any of you have thought of this dying thief only as one who put off repentance, I want you now to think of him as one who did greatly and grandly believe in Christ—and oh, that you would do the same! Oh, that you would put a great confidence in my great Lord! Never did a poor sinner trust Christ too much. There was never a case of a guilty one who believed Jesus could forgive him and afterward found that he could not—who believed that Jesus could save him on the spot and then woke up to find that it was a delusion. No, plunge into this river of confidence in Christ. The waters are waters to swim in, not to drown in. Never did a soul perish that glorified Christ by a living, loving faith in him. Come, then, with all your sin, whatever it may be, with all your deep depression of spirit, with all your agony of conscience. Come along with you and grasp my Lord and Master with both the hands of your faith, and he will be yours, and you will be his.

> Turn to Christ your longing eyes,
> View his bloody sacrifice:
> See in him your sins forgiven;
> Pardon, holiness, and heaven;
> Glorify the King of kings,
> Take the peace the gospel brings.

The Uniqueness of the Result of His Faith

I think I have shown you something special in the means of the thief's conversion and in his faith in our dying Lord. But now, as God may help me, I wish to show you another unique point— namely, in *the result of his faith*.

I have heard people say, "Well, you see, the dying thief was converted, but then he was not baptized. He never went to communion and never joined the church!" He could not do either! But that which God renders impossible to us, he does not demand of us. He was nailed to the cross; how could he be baptized? But he did a great deal more than that, for if he could not carry out the outward signs, he most manifestly exhibited the things that they signified, which, in his condition, was better still.

This dying thief first of all confessed the Lord Jesus Christ, and that is the very essence of baptism. He confessed Christ. Did he not acknowledge him to his fellow-thief? It was as open a confession as he could make it. Did he not acknowledge Christ before all who were gathered around the cross within hearing? It was as public a confession as he could possibly cause it to be. Yet certain cowardly fellows claim to be Christians, though they have never confessed Christ to a single person, and then they quote this poor thief as an excuse. Are they nailed to a cross? Are they dying in agony? Oh, no! And yet they talk as if they could claim the exemption these circumstances would give them. What a dishonest piece of business!

The fact is that our Lord requires an open confession as well as a secret faith. If you will not render it, there is no promise of salvation for you, but a threat of being denied at the last. The Apostle puts it this way: "If you confess with your mouth that Jesus is Lord and believe in your heart that God raised him from the dead, you will be saved" (Rom. 10:9). It is stated in another place upon this wise, "Whoever believes and is baptized will be saved" (Mark 16:16).

If there be a true faith, there must be a declaration of it. If you are candles, and God has lit you, "let your light shine before others, so that they may see your good works and give glory to your Father who is in heaven" (Matt. 5:16). Soldiers of Christ must, like her Majesty's soldiers, wear their regimentals; and if they are ashamed of their regimentals, they ought to be drummed out of the regiment. They are not honest soldiers who refuse to march in rank with their comrades. The very least thing the Lord Jesus Christ can expect of us is that we do confess him to the best of our power. If you are nailed up to a cross, I will not invite you to be baptized. If you are fastened up to a tree to die, I will not ask you to come into this pulpit and declare your faith, for you cannot. But you are required to do what you can do—namely, to make as distinct and open an avowal of the Lord Jesus Christ as may be suitable in your present condition.

I believe that many Christian people get into a deal of trouble through not being honest in their convictions. For instance, if a man goes into a workshop, or a soldier into a barrack-room, and if he does not fly his flag from the first, it will be very difficult for him to run it up afterward. But if he immediately and boldly lets them know, "I am a Christian man, and there are certain things I cannot do to please you, and certain other things I cannot help doing, though they displease you"—when that is clearly understood, after a while the singularity of the thing will be gone, and the man will be let alone. But if he is a little sneaky and thinks he is going to please the world and please Christ too, he is in for a rough time, let him depend upon it. His life will be that of a toad under a harrow or a fox in a dog kennel, if he tries the way of compromise. That will never do. Come out. Show your colors. Let it be known who you are and what you are. And although your course will not be smooth, it will certainly be not half so rough as if you tried to run with the hare and hunt with the hounds—a very difficult piece of business that. This man came out, then and there, and made as open an avowal of his faith in Christ as was possible.

The next thing the thief did was to rebuke his fellow-sinner. He spoke to him in answer to the ribaldry with which he had assailed our Lord. I do not know what the unconverted convict had been blasphemously saying, but his converted comrade spoke very honestly to him. "Do not you fear God, since you are under the same sentence of condemnation? And we indeed justly, for we are receiving the due reward of our deeds; but this man has done nothing wrong" (Luke 23:40–41). It is more than ever needful in these days that believers in Christ should not allow sin to go without rebuke—and yet a great many of them do so.

Do you not know that a person who is silent when a wrong thing is said or done may become a participator in the sin? If you do not rebuke sin—I mean, of course, on all fit occasions and in a proper spirit—your silence will give consent to the sin, and you will be an aider and abettor in it. A man who saw a robbery and who did not cry, "Stop thief!" would be thought to be in league with the thief. And the man who can hear swearing or see impurity and never utter a word of protest may well question whether he is right himself. Our "other men's sins" make up a great item in our personal guilt unless we in any way rebuke them. This our Lord expects us to do. The dying thief did it, and did it with all his heart, and therein far exceeded large numbers of those who hold their heads high in the church.

Next, the dying thief made a full confession of his guilt. He said to him who was hanged with him, "Do not you fear God, since you are under the same sentence of condemnation? And we indeed justly." Not many words, but what a world of meaning was in them—"we indeed justly." "You and I are dying for our crimes," he said, "and we deserve to die." When a man is willing to confess that he deserves the wrath of God—that he deserves the suffering that his sin has brought upon him—there is evidence of sincerity in him.

In this man's case, his repentance glittered like a holy tear in the eye of his faith so that his faith was bejeweled with the drops of his penitence. As I have often told you, I distrust the faith not born as a twin with repentance; but there is no room for suspicion in the case of this penitent confessor. I pray to God that you and I may have such a thorough work as this in our own hearts as the result of our faith.

Then, see, this dying thief defends his Lord. He says, "We indeed justly, . . . but this man has done nothing wrong." Was not that beautifully said? He did not say, "This man does not deserve to die," but "This man has done nothing wrong." He means that he is perfectly innocent. He does not even say, "He has done nothing wicked." But he asserts that he has not acted unwisely or indiscreetly: "This man has done nothing wrong."

This is a glorious testimony of a dying man to one who was numbered with the transgressors and was being put to death because his enemies falsely accused him. Beloved, I only pray that you and I may bear as good a witness to our Lord as this thief did. He outruns us all. We need not think much of the coming of his conversion late in life; we may far rather consider how blessed was the testimony he bore for his Lord when it was most needed. When all other voices were silent, one suffering penitent spoke out and said, "This man has done nothing wrong."

See, again, another mark of this man's faith. He prays, and his prayer is directed to Jesus. "Lord, remember me when you come into your kingdom." True faith is always praying faith. "Behold, he prays" is one of the surest tests of the new birth. Oh, friends, may we abound in prayer, for thus we must prove that our faith in Jesus Christ is what it ought to be! This converted robber opened his mouth wide in prayer. He prayed with great confidence as to the coming kingdom, and he sought that kingdom first, even to the exclusion of all else. He might have asked for life or for ease from pain, but he prefers the kingdom. This is a high mark of grace.

In addition to thus praying, you will see that he adores and worships Jesus, for he says, "Lord, remember me when you come into your kingdom." The petition is worded as if he felt, "Only let Christ think of me, and it is enough. Let him but remember me, and the thought of his mind will be effectual for everything I will need in the world to come." This is to impute Godhead to Christ.

If a man can cast his all upon the mere memory of a person, he must have a very high esteem of that person. If to be remembered by the Lord Jesus is all that this man asks or desires, he pays to the Lord great honor. I think there was about his prayer worship equal to the eternal hallelujahs of cherubim and seraphim. There was in it a glorification of his Lord not excelled even by the endless symphonies of angelic spirits who surround the throne. Thief, you have done well!

Oh, that some penitent spirit here might be helped thus to believe, thus, to confess, thus, to defend his Master, thus, to adore, thus, to worship; and then the age of the convert would be a matter of the smallest imaginable consequence.

The Uniqueness of What Was Gained

Now, the last remark is this: there was something very special about the dying thief as to our Lord's word to him about the world to come. He said to him, "Today you will be with me in paradise." He only asked the Lord to remember him, but he obtained this surprising answer, "Today you will be with me in paradise" (Luke 23:43).

In some respects, I envy this dying thief for this reason—that when the Lord pardoned me and pardoned the most of you who are present, he did not give us a place in paradise that same day. We are not yet come to the rest that is promised to us. No, you are waiting here.

Some of you have been waiting a long time. It is thirty years with many of us. It is forty years, fifty years, with many others since the Lord blotted out your sins, and yet you are not with him in paradise. There is a dear member of this church who, I suppose, has known the Lord for seventy-five years, and she is still with us, having long passed the ninetieth year of her age. The Lord did not admit her to paradise on the day of her conversion. He did not take any one of us from nature to grace, and from grace to glory, in a day. We have had to wait a good while. There is something for us to do in the wilderness, and so we are kept out of the heavenly garden.

I remember that Mr. [Richard] Baxter said that he was not in a hurry to be gone to heaven, and a friend called on John Owen, who had been writing about the glory of Christ, and asked him what he thought of going to heaven. That great divine replied, "I am longing to be there." "Why," said the other, "I have just spoken to holy Mr. Baxter, and he says that he would prefer to be here, since he thinks that he can be more useful on earth." "Oh!" said Dr. Owen, "my brother Baxter is always full of practical godliness, but for all that, I cannot say that I am at all desirous to linger in this mortal state. I would rather be gone."

Each of these men seems to me to have been the half of Paul. Paul was made up of the two, for he was desirous to depart, but he was willing to remain because it was needful for the people. We would put both together and, like Paul, have a strong desire to depart and to be with Christ, and yet be willing to wait, if we can do service to our Lord and to his church.

Still, I think he has the best of it who is converted and enters heaven the same night. This robber had breakfast with the devil but had lunch with Christ on earth and supper with him in paradise. This was short work but blessed work. What a host of troubles he escaped! What a world of temptation he missed! What an evil world he quitted! He was just born, like a lamb dropped in the field, and then he was lifted into the Shepherd's bosom straightaway.

I do not remember the Lord ever saying this to anybody else. I dare say it may have happened that souls have been converted and have gone home at once, but I never heard of anybody who had such an assurance from Christ as this man had: "Truly, I say to you." Such a personal assurance: "Truly, I say to you, today you will be with me in paradise." Dying thief, you were favored above many, to "be with Christ, for that is far better" (Phil. 1:23), and to be with him so soon!

Why is it that our Lord does not thus imparadise all of us at once? It is because there is something for us to do on earth. My brethren, are you doing it? Are you doing it? Some good people are still on earth—but why? But why? What is the use of them? I cannot make it out. If they are indeed the Lord's people, what are they here for? They get up in the morning and eat their breakfast, and in due course eat their dinner and their supper and go to bed and sleep. At a proper hour, they get up the next morning and do the same as on the previous day.

Is this living for Jesus? Is this life? Can this be the life of God in man? Oh, Christian people, do justify your Lord in keeping you waiting here! How can you justify him but by serving him to the utmost of your power? The Lord help you to do so! Why, you owe as much to him as the dying thief! I know I owe a great deal more. What a mercy it is to have been converted while you were yet a boy, to be brought to the Savior while you were yet a girl!

What a debt of obligation young Christians owe to the Lord! And if this poor thief crammed a life full of testimony into a few minutes, ought not you and I, who are spared, for years after conversion, to perform good service for our Lord? Come, let us wake up if we have been asleep! Let us begin to live if we have been half dead. May the Spirit of God make something of us yet, so that we may go as industrious servants from the labors of the vineyard to the pleasures of paradise! To our once crucified Lord be glory forever and ever! Amen.

Songs in the Night

Preached sometime in the mid to late 1800s.

But none says, "Where is God my Maker,
who gives songs in the night?"
Job 35:10

Elihu was a wise man. He was exceedingly wise, though not as wise as the all-wise Jehovah, who sees light in the clouds and finds order in confusion. Elihu was puzzled by Job's affliction. He pondered its cause. He wisely concluded that the most likely reason—though not the right one, in Job's case—is that it must have been because of Job's refusal to look to God: "Surely, if men be tried and troubled exceedingly, it is because, while they think about their troubles and distress themselves about their fears, they do not say, 'Where is God my Maker, who gives songs in the night?'"

Elihu's reason is the right assessment in the majority of cases. The great cause of the Christian's distress, the reason of the depths of sorrow into which many believers are plunged, is simply this—that while they are looking about, on the right hand and on the left, to see how they may escape their troubles, they forget to look to the hills from where all real help comes. They do not say, "Where is God my Maker, who gives songs in the night?" We will, however, leave that inquiry and dwell on those sweet words, "God my Maker, who gives songs in the night."

The world has its night. It seems necessary that it should have one. The sun shines by day, and men go forth to their labors while it is light. Men grow weary as the day lingers on. But as nightfall comes, like a sweet boon from heaven the darkness draws the curtains and shuts out the light, which might prevent our eyes from slumber. The sweet, calm stillness of the night permits us to rest upon the lap of ease and there forget our cares until the morning sun appears and an angel puts his hand on the curtain and undraws the curtain once again. As the day comes, the angel touches our eyelids and bids us rise and proceed to the labors of the day. Thus, night is one of the greatest blessings men enjoy. We have many reasons to thank God for it.

Night for many is a gloomy season. At night there is "the pestilence that stalks in darkness" (Ps. 91:6); there is "the terror of the night" (Ps. 91:5); there is the dread of robbers and all those fears that arise when there is no light to light our way. Night is the season of terror.

Yet even night has its songs. Have you never stood by the seaside at night and heard the pebbles sing and the waves chant God's glories? Or have you never risen from your bed, thrown up the window of your chamber, and listened there? Listened to what? Silence—save now and then a murmuring sound, which seems sweet music then. And have you not imagined that you heard the harp of God playing in heaven? Did you not conceive that the stars, that those eyes of God, looking down on you, were mouths full of song? Did you not conceive that every star was singing God's glory, singing, as it shone, of its mighty Maker? Night has its songs. We need not contain a poetic spirit to catch the song of night and hear the spheres as they chant the well-deserved praises of God. Though they be silent to the ear, they sing loudly the praises of the mighty God, who bears up the unpillared arch of heaven and moves the stars in their courses.

Man, too, like the great world in which he lives, must have his night. For it is true that man is like the world around him.

Man is a little world in that he resembles the world in almost everything. And if the world has its night, so man has his night. And many a night do we have—nights of sorrow, nights of persecution, nights of doubt, nights of bewilderment, nights of anxiety, nights of oppression, nights of ignorance, nights of all kinds, which press upon our spirits and terrify our souls. But, blessed be God, the Christian can say, "My God gives me songs in the night."

It is not necessary, I take it, to prove to you that Christians have nights. If you are Christian, then you will find that you have them. You don't need any proof, for nights come quite often enough. Because of this, I will proceed at once to the subject, and I will speak this evening on songs in the night: their source, their content, their excellence, and their uses.

The Source of Songs in the Night?

According to our text, "God" our "Maker" is the one who gives us a song in the night. Any man can sing in the day. When the cup is full, man draws inspiration from it; when wealth rolls in abundance, any man can sing to the praise of a God. It is easy enough for an Aeolian harp to whisper music when the winds blow; the difficulty is for music to come when no wind blows.

No man can make a song in the night himself. He may attempt it, but he will find the darkness too overwhelming. Let all things go as I please, and I will sing songs wherever I go. I can sing with the flowers growing on my path, but put me in a desert, where no flowers are, then how will I sing praises to God? Let this voice be free, let this body be full of health, then I can sing God's praises. But stop this tongue, lay me on the bed of languish, then it's not so easy to sing. Give me the bliss of spiritual liberty, and I will mount up with praises to my God, I will draw near to the throne, and I will sing, indeed, sing as sweet as seraphs. But confine me, fetter my spirit, clip my wings, make me exceedingly sad, so that I become old like the eagle—ah! then it is hard to sing.

It is not in man's power to sing when all is adverse. It is not natural to sing in trouble. "Bless the LORD, O my soul, and all that is within me, bless his holy name!" is a daylight song. But it was a divine song that Habakkuk sang, when in the night he said, "Though the fig tree shall not blossom, yet will I trust in the Lord, and stay myself in the God of Jacob." In the Red Sea any man could have made a song like that of Moses: "The horse and his rider he has thrown into the sea." The difficulty would have been to compose a song before the Red Sea had been divided and to sing it before Pharaoh's hosts had been drowned. It would have been difficult to have song while the darkness of doubt and fear was resting on Israel's hosts. Songs in the night come only from God for they are not in the power of man.

But what does the text mean when it asserts that God gives songs in the night? I think we find two answers to the question. First, I think, in the night of Christian experience, God is one's only. If it be daylight in my heart, I can sing songs touching my graces, songs touching my sweet experience, songs touching my duties, songs touching my labors. But let the night come, my graces appear to have withered; my evidences, though they are there, are hidden. I cannot

> read my title clear
> To mansions in the skies.

In the night I have nothing left to sing of but my God.

It is strange that when God gives his children mercies, they generally set their hearts more on the mercies than on the Giver of them. Yet when the night comes, and when God sweeps all the mercies away, then at once they say, "Now, my God, I have nothing to sing of but you. I must come to you; and to you alone. I had cisterns once that were full of water, but now the created streams are dry. Sweet Lord, I drink no stream but thine own self, I drink from no fount but from you."

Indeed, child of God, you know what I say; or if you don't understand, you will soon enough. It is in the night we sing of God, and of God alone. Every string is tuned, and every power has its part to sing, while we praise God and nothing else. We can make sacrifice to ourselves in day, but we only sacrifice to God by night. We can sing high praises to our dear selves when all is joyful, but we cannot sing praise to any save our God when circumstances and providences appear adverse. God alone can furnish us with songs in the night.

Second, not only does God give the song in the night, *he* is the only subject on which we can sing about in the night. Bring me a poor, melancholy, distressed child of God, and as I come into the pulpit, I will seek to tell him sweet promises and whisper to him sweet words of comfort. Yet, he will not listen to me. He is like the deaf adder; he listens not to the voice of the charmer. Send him to all the comforting divines and all the holy Barnabases who ever preached, and they will do very little—do as they may, they will not be able to squeeze a song out of him. He is drinking the gall of wormwood. He says, "O Lord, you have made me drunk with weeping; I have eaten ashes like bread." Comfort him as you may, it will be only a woeful note of mournful resignation that you will get from him. Though you will get no psalms of praise, no hallelujahs, no sonnets, let God come to this child in the night, let God whisper in his ear as he lies on his bed, and how you will see his eyes flash fire! Do you not hear him say?

> 'Tis paradise, if you are here;
> If you depart, 'tis hell.

I could not have cheered him, if God that has done it. It is God who "gives songs in the night." It is marvelous, brethren, how one sweet word of God will make whole songs for Christians. One word of God is like a piece of gold, and the Christian is the goldbeater, and he can hammer that promise out for weeks. I can say myself, I have lived on one promise for weeks, and want no other. I want to hammer that promise out into goldleaf and plate my whole existence with joy from it. The Christian gets his songs from God. God gives him inspiration and teaches him how to sing: "God my Maker, who gives songs in the night."

So, then, poor Christian, you need not go pumping up your poor heart to make it glad. Go to your Maker, and ask him to give you a song in the night. You are a poor dry well. You have heard it said that when a pump is dry, you must pour water down it first before you can expect water to flow up. And so, Christian, when you are dry, go to God and ask him to pour some joy down you, and then you will get some joy up from your own heart. Do not go to human comforters, for you will find them Job's comforters, but go first and foremost to your Maker, for he is the great composer of songs and teacher of music. He is the one who can teach you how to sing, "God, my Maker, who gives me songs in the night."

What Do We Sing About?

Why, I think, when we sing by night, there are three things we sing about. Either we sing about the yesterday that is over or about the night itself or about the tomorrow that is to come. Each of these are sweet themes when God our Maker gives us songs in the night.

We Can Sing about Yesterday

In the midst of the night, the most common theme for Christians to sing about is the day that is over. "Well," they say, "it is night now, but I can remember when it was daylight. Though neither moon nor stars appear now, I can remember when I saw the sun. I have no evidence at the moment, but there was a time when I could say, 'I know that my Redeemer lives.' I have my doubts and fears at this present moment, but it was not long ago that I could say, with full assurance, 'I know that he shed his blood for me; "For I know that my Redeemer lives, and at the last he will stand upon the earth. And after my skin has been thus destroyed, yet in my flesh I shall see God" (Job 19:25–27).' It may be darkness now, but I know the promises *were* sweet. I know I had blessed seasons in his house. I am quite sure of this. I used to enjoy myself in the ways of the Lord. And though now my paths are strewn with thorns, I know it is the King's highway. It was a way of pleasantness once; it will be a way of pleasantness again. 'I will remember the days of old; I will meditate on the years of the right hand of the Most High.'"

Christian, perhaps the best song you *can* sing to cheer you in the night is the song of yesterday. Remember, it was not always night with you; night is a new thing to you. Once you had a glad heart, a buoyant spirit. Once your eye was full of fire. Once your foot was light. Once you could sing for joy and ecstasy of heart. Well, then, remember that God, who made you sing yesterday, has not left you in the night. He is not a daylight God, who cannot know his children in darkness, but he loves you now as much as ever. Though he has left you a little, it is to prove you, to make you trust him better and serve him more. Let me tell you some of the sweet things of which a Christian may make a song when he is in the night.

If we are going to sing of the things of yesterday, let us begin with what God has done for us. My beloved brethren, you will find it a sweet subject for a song to sing of electing love and covenanted mercies. When you yourself are low, it is well to sing of the fountainhead of mercy, of that blessed decree wherein you were ordained to eternal life and of that glorious Man who undertook your redemption, of that solemn covenant signed and sealed and ratified. In the night, you can sing of God's everlasting love that chose you before the snow-capped mountains were begotten. You can sing of the electing love that loved you firmly, loved you fast, loved you well, and loved you eternally.

I tell you, believer, if you can go back to the years of eternity—if you can in your mind run back to that time before the everlasting hills were fashioned and the fountains of the great deep scooped out, and if you can see your God inscribing your name in his eternal Book—if you can read in his loving heart eternal thoughts of love to you, you will find this a charming means of giving you songs in the night. No lyrics are as sweet as those which come from electing love, no sonnets like those that are dictated by meditations on discriminating mercy.

Think, Christian, of the eternal covenant, and you will get a song in the night. But if you do not have a voice tuned to so high a key as that, let me suggest some other mercies you may sing about—and they are the mercies you have experienced. What, man! can you not sing a little of that blessed hour when Jesus met you, when you were a blind slave sporting with death, and he saw you and said: "Come, poor slave, come with me"? Can you not sing of that rapturous moment when he snapped your fetters, dashed your chains to the earth, and said, "I am the Breaker; I came to break your chains and set you free"? Though you are ever so gloomy now, can you forget that happy morning when, in the house of God, your voice was loud, almost as a seraph's voice, in praise, for you could sing, "I am forgiven! I am forgiven; a monument of grace, a sinner saved by blood"? Go back, man; sing of that moment, and then you will have a song in the night.

Or if you have almost forgotten that, then surely you had some precious milestone along the road of life that is not quite grown over with moss, on which you can read some happy inscription of his mercy toward you! What! did you ever have a sickness like that which you are suffering now, and did he not raise you up from that? Were you never poor before, and did he not supply your wants? Were you never in straits before, and did he not deliver you? Come, man! I beseech you, go to the river of your experience, and pull up a few bulrushes, and weave them into an ark in which your infant faith may float safely on the stream.

I bid you not forget what God has done for you. What! have you buried your own diary? I beseech you, man, turn over the book of your remembrance. Can you not see some sweet hill Mizar? Can you not think of some blessed hour when the Lord met with you at Hermon? Have you never been on the Delectable Mountains? Have you never been brought out from the den of lions? Have you never escaped the jaw of the lion and the paw of the bear? No, O man, I know you have. Go back, then, a little way, and take the mercies of the past, and though it is dark now, light up the lamps of yesterday, and they will glitter through the darkness, and you will find that God has given you a song in the night.

"Indeed," says one, "but you know that when we are in the dark, we cannot see the mercies God has given us. It is all very well for you to tell us this, but we cannot get hold of them." I remember an old experienced Christian speaking about the great pillars of our faith. He was a sailor, and we were on board ship as we observed the huge posts on the shore that were used to tie off boats. After I had sought to encourage him with the many promises of the Bible, he said, "I know they are good, strong promises, but I cannot get near enough to shore to throw my rope around them—that is the difficulty." Now, it often happens that God's past mercies and lovingkindnesses would be good, sure posts to hold on to, but we have not got faith enough to throw our ropes around them. And so, we go slipping down the stream of unbelief because we cannot sustain ourselves on our former mercies.

I will, however, give you something I think you can throw your rope over. If God has never been kind to you, one thing you surely know, and that is, he has been kind to others. Come, now; if you are in ever so great straits, sure there were others in greater straits. What! are you lower than poor Jonah when he went down to the bottoms of the mountains? Are you poorer than your Master when he had not a place where to lay his head? What! Do you conceive yourself to be the worst of the worst? Look at Job there scraping himself with a potsherd and sitting on a dunghill. Are you as bad as he? And yet Job rose up and was richer than before; and out of the depths Jonah came and preached the Word; and our Savior Jesus has mounted to his throne!

O Christian! only think of what God has done for others! If you cannot remember God doing anything for you, yet remember, I beseech you, what his usual rule is, and do not judge my God to be unmerciful. You remember when Benhadad was overcome and fled, and his servants said to him, "Behold now, we have heard that the kings of the house of Israel are merciful kings. Let us put sackcloth around our waists and ropes on our heads and go out to the king of Israel. Perhaps he will spare your life." Benhadad sent to the king; he had received no kindness from Ahab before but had only heard that he was a merciful king. So, to the king he went, and what did the king say? "Is he yet alive? He is my brother!" Truly, poor soul, if you have never had a merciful God, yet others have; the King is a merciful king. Go and try him. If you are ever so low in your troubles, look to the hills, from where your help comes. Others have had help there, and so may you.

Hundreds of God's children might show us their hands full of comforts and mercies of God. And all these Christians would say, "The Lord gave us these without money and without price; and why should he not give to you also, since you too are the King's son?" Thus, Christian, you will get a song in the night out of other people, if you can't get a song from yourself.

Never be ashamed of taking a page out of another man's experience book. If you can't find a good page in your own, tear one out of someone else's. And if you have no cause to be grateful to God in darkness, or cannot find cause in your own experiences, go to someone else, and if you can, harp God's praise in the dark and, like the nightingale, sing his praise sweetly when all the world has gone to rest. Sing in the night of the mercies of yesterday

We Can Sing about the Night

But I think, beloved, there is never so dark a night that we can't find something to sing about. For there is one thing I am sure we can sing about, let the night be ever so dark, and even then "it is of the Lord's mercies that we are not consumed, and because his compassions fail not." If we cannot sing very loudly, we can still sing a little low tune, something like this: "He does not deal with us according to our sins, nor repay us according to our iniquities."

"Oh," says one, "I do not know where to get food for tomorrow. I am a poor wretch." So, you may be, my dear friend, but you are not so poor as you deserve to be. Do not be mightily offended about that. If you are, you are no child of God, for the child of God acknowledges that he has no right to the least of God's mercies. Every mercy comes through the channel of grace alone. As long as I am out of hell, I have no right to grumble. If I were in hell, I should have no right to complain, for I feel, when convinced of sin, that never a creature deserved to go there more than I do. We have no cause to murmur. We can lift up our hands and say, "Night! you are dark, but you might have been darker. I am poor, but if I could not have been poorer, I might have been sick. I am poor and sick—well, I have some friends left; my lot can't be so bad. It could be worse."

And therefore, Christian, you will always have one thing to sing about: "Lord, I thank you, it is not all darkness!" Besides, Christian, however dark the night is, there is always a star or moon. There is scarce ever a night that we have, but there are just one or two little lamps burning up there. However dark it may be, I think you may find some little comfort, some little joy, some little mercy left, and some little promise to cheer your spirit. The stars are not put out, are they? No, if you cannot see them, they are there; at least one or two are shining upon you. Therefore, give God a song in the night. If you have only one star, bless God for that one—perhaps he will make it two. And if you have only two stars, bless God twice for the two stars, and perhaps he will make them four. Try, then, to see if you cannot find a song in the night.

We Can Sing about Tomorrow

But, beloved, there is another thing of which we can sing yet more sweetly, and that is, we can sing of the day that is to come. Often do I cheer myself with the thought of the coming of the Lord. We preach now, perhaps, with little success; "the kingdoms of this world" have not yet "become the kingdoms of our Lord and of his Christ." We send out missionaries; they are for the most part unsuccessful. We are laboring, but we do not see the fruit of our labors. Well, what then? We will not always labor in vain or spend our strength for nothing. A day is coming, and now is, when every minister of Christ will speak with unction, when all the servants of God will preach with power, and when colossal systems of heathenism will tumble from their pedestals, and mighty, gigantic delusions will be scattered to the winds.

The shout will be heard, "Alleluia! Alleluia! The Lord God Omnipotent reigns." I look for that day. It is to the bright horizon of the second coming of Christ that I turn my eyes.

My anxious expectation is that the sweet Sun of righteousness will arise with healing beneath his wings, that the oppressed will be righted, that despotism will be cut down, that liberty will be established, that peace will be made lasting, and that the glorious liberty of the gospel of God will be extended throughout the known world. Christian! if it is night with you, think of tomorrow. Cheer your heart with the thought of the coming of your Lord. Be patient, for you know who has said, "Behold, I am coming soon, bringing my recompense with me, to repay each one for what he has done."

One thought more upon that point. There is another sweet tomorrow of which we hope to sing in the night. Soon, beloved, you and I will lie on our deathbed, and we will want a song in the night then. And I do not know where we will get it, if we do not get it from tomorrow. Last night, as I was kneeling by the bed of an apparently dying saint, I said, "Well, sister, he has been precious to you; you can rejoice in his covenant mercies and his past lovingkindnesses." She put out her hand, and said, "Ah! sir, do not talk about them now; I want the sinner's Savior as much now as ever. It is not a saint's Savior I want; it is still a sinner's Savior I am in need of, for I am a sinner still." I found that I could not comfort her with the past, so I reminded her of the golden streets, of the gates of pearl, of the walls of jasper, of the harps of gold, of the songs of bliss. Then her eye glistened, and she said, "Yes, I shall be there soon. I shall meet them by-and-by," and then she seemed so joyful!

Ah! believer, you may always cheer yourself with that thought; for if you are ever so low now, remember that "a few more rolling suns, at most, will land you on fair Canaan's coast." Your head may be crowned with thorny troubles now, but it will wear a starry crown directly. Your hand may be filled with cares, but it will grasp a harp soon, a harp full of music. Your garments may be soiled with dust now, but they will be white soon enough. Wait a little longer. Ah! beloved, how despicable our troubles and trials will seem when we look back upon them! Looking at them here in the present, they seem immense, but when we get to heaven, we will then, "with transporting joys, recount the labors of our feet."

Our trials will seem to us nothing at all. We will talk to one another about them in heaven, and find all the more to converse about, according as we have suffered more here below. Let us go on, therefore, and if the night be ever so dark, remember there is not a night that will not have a morning, and that morning is to come eventually. When sinners are lost in darkness, *we* will lift up our eyes in everlasting light. Surely, I need not dwell longer on this thought. There is matter enough for songs in the night— in the past, the present, and the future.

What Makes This Song So Glorious?

In the first place, when you hear a man singing a song in the night—I mean in the night of trouble—you may be quite sure it is a hearty one. Many of you sang beautifully just a while ago, didn't you? I wonder whether you would sing just as beautifully if there were a stake or two in Smithfield for all of you who dared to do it?[1] If you sang under pain and penalty, that would show your song is in your heart. We can all sing very nicely indeed when everybody else sings. It is the easiest thing in the world to open your mouth and let the words come out, but when the devil puts his hand over your mouth, can you sing then? Can you say, "Though he slay me, yet will I trust in him"? That is hearty singing. That is a real song that springs up in the night.

The nightingale sings most sweetly because she sings in the night. We know a poet has said that if she sings by day, she might be thought to sing no more sweetly than the wren. It is the stillness of the night that makes her song sweet. And so does a Christian's song become sweet and hearty because it is in the night.

Again, the songs we sing in the night will be *lasting*. Many

---

1 Smithfield, London, was a place of execution, where three hundred Protestants were martyred, burnt at the stake, during the reign of "Bloody Mary."

songs we hear our fellow creatures singing in the streets will not do to sing in the eternal state. I guess they will sing a different kind of tune soon. Now they can sing any boisterous drinking songs, but they will not sing them when they come to die. They are not exactly the songs with which to cross Jordan's billows. It will not do to sing one of those light songs when death and you are having the last tug. It will not do to enter heaven singing one of those unchaste, unholy sonnets.

No! But the Christian who can sing in the night will not have to stop his song; he may keep on singing it forever. He may put his foot in Jordan's stream and continue his melody. He may wade through it and keep on singing and land himself safely in heaven. And when he is there, there will be no need for a gap in his strain, but in a nobler, sweeter strain, he may still continue singing the Savior's power to save.

There are a great many of you who think Christian people are very miserable, don't you? You say, "Let me sing my song." Aye, but, my dear friends, we like to sing a song that will last. We don't like your songs; they are all froth, like bubbles on the breaker, and they will soon die away and be lost. Give me a song that will last; give me one that will not melt. Oh, give me not the dreamer's gold! He hoards it up, and says, "I'm rich," and when he wakes, his gold is gone. But give me songs in the night, for they are songs I sing forever.

Again, the songs we warble in the night are those that show we have *real faith* in God. Many men have just enough faith to trust God as far as they can see him, and they always sing as far as they can see providence go right. But true faith can sing when it cannot see. It can take hold of God when they cannot discern him.

Songs in the night, too, prove that we have *true courage*. Many people sing by day who are silent by night. They are afraid of thieves and robbers. Yet the Christian who sings in the night proves himself to be a courageous character. It is the bold Christian who can sing God's sonnets in the darkness.

He who can sing songs in the night proves also that he has

true love to Christ. It is not love to Christ to praise him while everybody else praises him—to walk arm in arm with him when he has the crown on his head is no great deed. To believe in Christ when he is shrouded in darkness, to stick hard and fast by the Savior when all men speak ill of him and forsake him, that is true faith. He who sings a song to Christ in the night sings the best song in all the world, for he sings from the heart.

What Are the Benefits of This Song?

Well, beloved, it is very useful to sing in the night of our troubles, first, *because it will cheer ourselves.* When you were boys living in the country and had some distance to go alone at night, don't you remember how you whistled and sang to keep your courage up? Well, what we do in the natural world we ought to do in the spiritual. There is nothing like singing to keep your spirits alive.

When we have been in trouble, we have often thought ourselves to be nearly overwhelmed with difficulty, and we have said, "Let us have a song." We have begun to sing, and we proved what Martin Luther said, "The devil cannot bear singing." That is about the truth; he does not like music. It was so in Saul's days as an evil spirit rested on Saul, but when David played on his harp, the evil spirit went away from him. This is usually the case. If we can begin to sing, we must remove our fears. I like to hear servants sometimes humming a tune at their work. I love to hear a plowman in the county singing as he goes along with his horses. Why not? You say he has no time to praise God, but he can sing a song—surely, he can sing a psalm, for it will take no more time. Singing is the best thing to purge ourselves of evil thoughts. Keep your mouth full of songs, and you will often keep your heart full of praises. Keep on singing as long as you can, and you will find it a good method of driving away your fears.

Sing in trouble, again, because *God loves to hear his people sing in the night.* At no time does God love his children's singing so well as when they give a serenade of praise under his window, when he has hidden his face from them. They are all in darkness, but they come under his window, and they begin to sing there.

"Ah!" says God, "that is true faith that can make them sing praises when I will not look at them. I know there is some faith in them that makes them lift up their hearts even when I seem to take away all my tender mercies and all my compassions."

Sing, Christian, for singing pleases God. In heaven, we read, the angels are employed in singing. You too should be employed in the same activity. By no better means can you gratify the Almighty One of Israel, who stoops from his high throne to observe the poor creature of a day.

Sing, again, for another reason: because *it will cheer your companions.* If any of them are in the valley and in the darkness with you, it will be a great help to comfort them. John Bunyan tells us that as Christian was going through the valley, he found it a dreadful dark place. The valley was full of terrible demons and goblins. And poor Christian thought he was most certainly going to perish. But just when his doubts were the strongest, he heard a sweet voice. He listened to it, and he heard a man in front of him saying, "Yea, when I pass through the valley of the shadow of death, I will fear no evil." Now, that man did not know who was near him, but he was unwittingly singing to cheer a man behind.

Christian, when you are in trouble, sing; you do not know who is near you. Sing! Perhaps you will get a good companion by it. Sing! Perhaps there will be many a heart cheered by your song. There is some broken spirit, it may be, that will be bound up by your sonnets. Sing! There is some poor distressed brother, perhaps, shut up in the Castle of Despair, who, like King Richard, will hear your song inside the walls, and sing to you again, and you may be the means of getting him a ransom and released.[2]

Sing, Christian, wherever you go. Try, if you can, to wash your face every morning in a bath of praise. When you go down from your bedroom, never go to look on man until you have first looked on your God. When you have looked on him, seek to come down with a face beaming with joy. Carry a smile, for you

---

2   King Richard I (1157–1199) of England was captured and imprisoned in Dürn-
stein Castle in Austria for a time when he was returning from the Third Crusade.

will cheer up many a poor wayworn pilgrim by it. And when you fast, when you have an aching heart, do not appear to men to fast. Rather, appear cheerful and happy. Anoint your head and wash your face. Be happy for your brother's sake—it will tend to cheer him up and help him through the valley.

One more reason, and I know it will be a good one for you. Try and sing in the night, Christian, for *that is one of the best arguments in all the world for Christian faith.* Theologians spend a lot of time trying to prove Christianity. I should like to have seen Paul trying that! Elymas the sorcerer withstood him. How did our friend Paul treat him? He said, "You son of the devil, you enemy of all righteousness, full of all deceit and villainy, will you not stop making crooked the straight paths of the Lord?" That is about the politeness such men ought to have who deny God's truth. We must start with this assumption: we may prove that the Bible is God's word, but we are not going to prove God's word. If you do not like to believe it, we will shake hands and bid you goodbye. We will not argue with you. Christianity is not a thing merely for your intellect to prove the greatness of your own talent; it is a thing that demands your faith. As a messenger of heaven, I demand that faith. If you do not choose to give it, then you are responsible for your own doom.

Oh, Christian, instead of disputing, let me tell you how to prove your faith. Live it out! live it out! Give the external as well as the internal evidence. When you are sick, let your neighbor, who laughs at Christianity, come into your house. When he was sick, he said, "Oh, send for the doctor," and there he was fretting and fuming and whining and making all manner of noises. When you are sick, send for him. Tell him that you are resigned to the Lord's will, that you will kiss the chastening rod, that you will take the cup and drink it because your Father gives it. You need not make a boast of this, or it will lose all its power. But do it because you cannot help doing it. Your neighbor will say, "There is something to his faith." And when you come to the borders of the grave—he was there once, and you heard how he shrieked and how frightened he was—give him your hand, and say to him, "Ah! I have a Christ; I have a faith that will make me sing in the night." Let him hear how you can sing, "Victory, victory, victory!"

I tell you; we may preach fifty thousand sermons to prove the gospel, but we will not prove it half so well as you will through singing in the night. Keep a cheerful frame, keep a happy heart, keep a contented spirit, keep your eye up and your heart aloft, and you will prove Christianity better than all the Butlers and all the wise men who ever lived. Give them the analogy of a holy life, and then you will prove Christianity to them. Give them the evidence of internal piety, developed externally, and you will give the best possible proof of Christianity. Try and sing songs in the night, for they are so rare that, if you can sing them, you will honor your God and bless your friends.

I have been preaching all this to the children of God, and now there is a sad turn that this subject must take, just one moment or so, and then we will be done. There is a night coming in which there will be no songs of joy—a night in which no one will even attempt to lead a chorus. There is a night coming when a song will be sung, of which misery will be the subject, set to the music of wailing and gnashing of teeth. There is a night coming when woe—unutterable woe—will be the matter of an awful terrific *miserere*—when the orchestra will be composed of damned men and howling fiends and yelling demons.

I speak what I know, and testify to the Scriptures. There is a night coming for a poor soul within this house tonight, and unless he repents, it will be a night wherein he will have to growl and howl and sigh and cry and moan and groan forever. "Who is that?" you ask. Yourself, my friend, if you are godless and Christless. "What!" you say, "am I in danger of hellfire?" In danger, my friend! Indeed, more—you are damned already. So says the Bible. You say, "And can you leave me without telling me what I must do to be saved? Can you believe that I am in danger of perishing and not speak to me?" I trust not; I hope I will never preach a sermon without speaking to the ungodly, for oh! how I love them.

Swearer, your mouth is black with oaths now, and if you die, you must go on blaspheming throughout eternity. But listen to me, blasphemer! Do you repent tonight? Do you feel yourself to have sinned against God? Do you feel a desire to be saved? Listen, you may be saved. You may be saved as much as anyone who is now here.

There is another: she has sinned against God enormously, and she blushes even now while I mention her case. Do you repent of your sin? There is hope for you. Remember him who said, "Go, and sin no more."

Drunkard! But a little while ago you were reeling down the street, and now you repent. Drunkard! There is hope for you. "Well," you ask, "What must I do to be saved?" Then again let me tell you the old way of salvation. It is "Believe in the Lord Jesus Christ, and you are saved." We can get no further than that, do what we will; this is the sum and substance of the gospel. Believe in the Lord Jesus Christ, and be baptized, and you will be saved. So says the Scripture.

Do you ask, "What is it to believe?" Am I to tell you again? I cannot tell you, except that it is to look at Christ. Do you see that Savior there? He is hanging on the cross; there are his dear hands, pierced with nails, nailed to a tree, as if they were waiting for your tardy footsteps, because you would not come. Do you see his dear head there? It is hanging on his breast, as if he would lean over and kiss your poor soul. Do you see his blood gushing from his head, his hands, his feet, his side? It is running after you. It is running after you because he well knew that you would never run after it. Sinner! To be saved, all you have to do is look at that Man. Can you not do it now?

"No," you say, "I do not believe it will save me." Ah! my poor friend, try it, and if you do not succeed when you have tried it, I am bondsman for my Lord—here, take me, bind me, and I will suffer your doom for you. This I will venture to say: if you cast yourself on Christ and he doesn't forgive you, I will be willing to go halves with you in all your misery and woe. For he will never do it: never, *never*, NEVER!

No sinner was ever empty sent back,
who came seeking mercy for Jesus' sake.

I plead with you, therefore, try him, and you will not try him in vain but will find him "able to save to the uttermost those who draw near to God through him." You will be saved now and saved forever.

May God give you his blessing! I cannot preach as earnestly as I could wish, but nevertheless, may God accept these words and send them home to some hearts this night! And may you, my dear brothers and sisters, have songs in the night!

The Raven's Cry

No. 672, Metropolitan Tabernacle, London, England
January 14, 1866

He gives to the beasts their food, and to the
young ravens that cry.
– Psalm 147:9

I will open this sermon with a quotation. I must give you, in Caryl's own words, his note about ravens:

> Naturalists tell us that ravens fed their young in the nest until they are able to fly abroad. They then thrust their young out of the nest and will not let them return. When these young ravens are on their first flight and little acquainted with how to feed themselves, then the Lord provides food for them. It is said by credible authorities that ravens are strict and severe in this, for as soon as their young are able to provide for themselves, they will not gather any more food for them. And some affirm the old ones will not allow the young ravens to stay in the same area where they were bred, and if so, then they must

wander. We say proverbially, "Need makes the old wife trot"; we may say, "and the young ones too." It has been, and possibly is, the practice of some parents to turn their children out as soon as they are able to provide for themselves. Now, said the Lord in the text, when the young ravens are in this pinch, when they are turned away from their nest to wander and look for their own food, who then provides for them? Do not I, the Lord? Do not I provide for the old raven and his young ones, both while they remain in the nest and when they wander for lack of food?

Solomon sent the sluggard to the ant, and taught himself lessons from conies, greyhounds, and spiders. Let us be willing to be instructed by any of God's creatures, and go to the ravens' nest tonight to learn as in a school.

To the pure, nothing is unclean, and to the wise, nothing is trivial. Let the superstitious dread the raven as a bird of ill omen and let the thoughtless see nothing but a winged thing in glossy black. We are willing to see more and doubtless will not be unrewarded if we are but teachable. Noah's raven brought him back no olive branch, but ours may tonight, and it may even come to pass that ravens may bring us food tonight as of old they fed Elijah by Cherith's brook.

Our blessed Lord once derived a very potent argument from ravens—an argument intended to comfort and cheer those of his servants who were oppressed with needless anxieties about their temporal circumstances. To such he said, "Consider the ravens: they neither sow nor reap, they have neither storehouse nor barn, and yet God feeds them. Of how much more value are you than the birds!" (Luke 12:24).

Following the Master's logic—which you will all agree must have been sound, for he was never untruthful in his reasoning any more than in his statements—I will argue tonight in this way: Consider the ravens as they cry; with harsh, inarticulate, croaking notes they make known their wants, and your heavenly

Father answers their prayer and sends them food. You, too, have begun to pray and to seek his favor. Are you not much better than they? Does God care for ravens, and will he not care for you? Does he listen to the cries of the unfledged ravens in their nests, when hungry they cry unto him and watch to be fed?

Does he, I say, supply them in answer to their cries, and will he not answer you, poor trembling children of men, who are seeking his face and favor through Christ Jesus? The whole business of this evening will be just simply to work that one thought out. I will aim tonight, under the guidance of the Holy Spirit, to say something to those praying for mercy but as yet have not received it, who have gone on their knees, perhaps for months, with one exceedingly great and bitter cry, but as of yet know not the way of peace.

Their sin still hangs like a millstone about their neck. They sit in the valley of the shadow of death. No light has dawned upon them, and they are wringing their hands and moaning, "Has God forgotten to be gracious? Has he shut his ear against the prayers of seeking souls? Will he be mindful of sinners' piteous cries no more? Will penitents' tears drop upon the earth and no longer move his compassion?" Satan, too, is telling you, dear friends, who are now in this state of mind, that God will never hear you, that he will let you cry until you die, that you will pant out your life in sighs and tears, and that at the end you will be cast into the lake of fire.

I long tonight to give you some comfort and encouragement. I want to urge you to cry yet more vehemently. Come to the cross and lay hold of it, and vow that you will never leave its shadow until you find the gift your soul covets. I want to move you, if God the Holy Spirit will help me, so that you will say within yourselves, like Queen Esther, "I will go to the King, and if I perish, I perish." And may you add to that the vow of Jacob, "I will not let you go, except you bless me!"

If God Hears the Ravens, Will He Not Hear You?

I argue that he will, first, when I remember that he hears the lowly raven cry, and that you, in some sense, are much better than a raven.

The raven is but a poor unclean bird, whose instant death would make no sort of grievous gap in creation. If thousands of ravens had their necks wrung tomorrow, I do not know that there would be any vehement grief and sorrow in the universe about them. It would simply be a number of poor dead birds, and that would be all. But you are an immortal soul. The raven is gone when life is over; there is no raven any longer. But when your present life is past, you have not ceased to be. You are but launched upon the sea of life; you have but begun to live forever.

You will see earth's snowy mountains crumble to nothingness before your immortal spirit will expire. The moon will have paled her feeble light, and the sun's fires will have been quenched in perpetual darkness, and yet your spirit will still be marching on in its everlasting course—an everlasting course of misery, unless God hears your cry.

> Oh, that truth immense,
> This mortal, immortality shall wear!
> The pulse of mind shall never cease to play;
> By God awakened, it forever throbs,
> Eternal as his own eternity!
> Above the angels, or below the fiends:
> To mount in glory, or in shame descend—
> Mankind is destined by resistless doom.

Do you think, then, that God will hear the poor bird that is and is not, and is here a moment and is blotted out of existence, and will he not hear you, an immortal soul, whose duration is to be co-equal with his own? I think it surely must strike you that if he hears the dying raven, he will also hear an undying man. The ancients said of Jupiter that he was not at leisure to mind little things, but Jehovah condescends to care for the least of his creatures, and even looks into birds' nests. Will he not mercifully care for spirits who are heirs of a dread eternity?

Moreover, I never heard of ravens that they were made in the image of God, but I do find that, defiled, deformed, and debased as our race is, originally God said, "Let us make man in our own image." There is something about man that is not to be found in the lower creatures, the best and noblest of whom are immeasurably beneath the meanest child of Adam. A council was held as to the creation of man, and in his mind, and even in the adaptation of his body to assist the mind, there is a marvelous display of the wisdom of the Most High. Bring here the most deformed, obscure, and wicked of the human race, and though I dare not flatter human nature morally, yet there is a dignity about the fact of mankind that is not to be found in all the beasts of the field, be they what they may.

Behemoth and Leviathan are put in subjection beneath the foot of man. The eagle cannot soar as high as man's soul mounts, nor the lion feed on such royal meat as man's spirit hungers after. And do you think that God will hear so low and so mean a creature as a raven, and yet not hear you, when you are one of those he formed in his own image? Oh! think not so harshly and so foolishly of him whose ways are always equal!

I will put this to yourselves. Does not nature itself teach that man is to be cared for above the birds of the air? If you heard the cries of young ravens, you might feel compassion enough for those birds to give them food, if you knew how to feed them. But I cannot believe that any of you would help the birds and yet would not fly upon the wings of compassion to the rescue of a perishing infant whose cries you might hear from the place where it was cast by cruel neglect. If, in the stillness of the night, you heard the plaintive cry of a man dying in sickness, unpitied in the streets, would you not arise and help him? I am sure you would if you are one who would help a raven. If you have any compassion for a raven, surely much more would you have pity on a man.

I know it is whispered that some simpletons care more for homeless dogs than for homeless men and women, and yet it is far more probable that those who feel for dogs are those who care most tenderly for men. At any rate, I should feel a strong presumption in their favor if I needed aid. And do you not think that God, the All-Wise One, when he cares for these unfledged birds in the nest, will be sure also to care for you? Your heart says yes—then from now on answer the unbelief of your heart by turning its own just reasoning against it.

But I hear you say, "Ah! but the raven is not sinful as I am. It may be an unclean bird, but it cannot be so unclean as I am morally. It may be black in hue, but I am black with sin. A raven cannot break the Sabbath, cannot swear, cannot commit adultery. A raven cannot be a drunkard, it cannot defile itself with vices such as those with which I am polluted." I know all that, friend, and it may seem to you to make your case more hopeless, but I do not think it does so really.

Just think of it for a minute. What does this prove? Why, that you are a creature capable of sinning and, consequently, that you are an intelligent spirit living in a sense in which a raven does not live. You are a creature moving in the spirit world. You belong to the world of souls in which the raven has no portion. The raven cannot sin because it has no spirit, no soul. But you are an intelligent agent of which the better part is your soul.

Now, as the soul is infinitely more precious than the body, and as the raven—I am speaking popularly now—is nothing but body, while you are evidently soul as well as body, or else you would not be capable of sinning, I see even in that black discouraging thought some gleam of light. Does God care for flesh and blood and bones and black feathers, and will he not care for your reason, your will, your judgment, your conscience, your immortal soul?

Oh, if you will but think of it, you must see that it is not possible for a raven's cry to gain an audience of the ear of divine benevolence, and yet for your prayer to be despised and disregarded by the Most High.

> The insect that with puny wing,
> Just shoots along one summer's ray;
> The flower which the breath of Spring
> Wakes into life for half a day;
> The smallest mote, the most tenderest hair,
> All feel our heavenly Father's care.

Surely, then, he will have respect for the cry of the humble and will not refuse their prayer. I can hardly leave this point without remarking that the mention of a raven should encourage a sinner. As an old author writes,

> Among fowls he does not mention the hawk or falcon, which are highly prized and fed by princes, nor the sweet singing nightingale, or such like musical pretty birds, which men keep choicely and much delight in, but he chooses that hateful and malicious bird, the croaking raven, whom no man values but as she eats up the carrion which might annoy him.
>
> Behold then, and wonder at the providence and kindness of God, that he should provide food for the raven, a creature of so dismal a hue, and of so un-tunable a tone, a creature that is so odious to most men, and ominous to some. There is a great providence of God seen in providing for the ant, who gathers her food in summer, but a greater in the raven, who, though he forgets, or is careless to provide for himself, yet God provides and lays up for him.
>
> One would think the Lord should say of ravens, "Let them shift for themselves or perish." No, the Lord God does not despise any work of his hands. The raven has his being from God, and therefore the raven will be provided for by him. Not only the fair innocent dove but the ugly raven has his meat from God, which clearly shows that the lack of excellence in you, you black, raven-like sinner, will not prevent your cry from being heard in heaven.

The blood of Jesus will remove unworthiness, and he will utterly cleanse away defilement. Only believe on Jesus, and you will find peace.

There Is a Difference Between You and a Raven

When the young ravens cry, I suppose they scarcely know what they want. They have a natural instinct that makes them cry for food, but their cry does not in itself express their want. You would soon find out, I suppose, that they meant food, but they have no articulate speech. They do not utter so much as a single word. It is just a constant, croaking, craving cry, and that is all. But you do know what you want, and few as your words are, your heart knows its own bitterness and dire distress. Your sighs and groans have an obvious meaning. Your understanding is at the right hand of your necessitous heart.

You know that you want—peace and pardon. You know that you need Jesus, his precious blood, his perfect righteousness. Now, if God hears such a strange, chattering, indistinct cry as that of a raven, don't you think he will also hear the rational and expressive prayer of a poor, needy, guilty soul who is crying unto him, "God be merciful to me a sinner"? Surely your reason tells you that!

Moreover, the young ravens cannot use arguments, for they have no understanding. They cannot say as you can,

> He knows what arguments I'd take
> To wrestle with my God,
> I'd plead for his own mercy's sake,
> And for a Savior's blood.

They have one argument, namely, their dire necessity, which forces their cry from them, but beyond this they cannot go, and even this they cannot set forth in order, or describe in language. But you have a multitude of arguments ready at hand, and you have an understanding with which to set them in array and marshal them to besiege the throne of grace. Surely, if the mere plea of the unuttered want of the raven prevails with God, much more will you prevail with the Most High, if you can argue your case before him and come to him with arguments in your mouth.

Come, you who are despairing, and try my Lord! I do beseech you now, let that doleful ditty ascend into the ears of mercy! Open that bursting heart, and let it out in tears, if words are beyond your power.

A raven, however, I fear, has sometimes a great advantage over some sinners who seek God in prayer, namely in this—*young ravens are more in earnest about their food than some are about their souls.* This, however, is no discouragement to you, but rather a reason why you should be more earnest than you have been. When ravens want food, they do not cease crying until they've gotten it. There is no quieting a hungry young raven until his mouth is full, and there is no quieting a sinner when he is really in earnest until he gets his heart full of divine mercy.

I would that some of you prayed more vehemently! "The kingdom of heaven has suffered violence, and the violent take it by force" (Matt. 11:12). An old Puritan said, "Prayer is a cannon set at the gate of heaven to burst open its gates." You must take the city by storm if you would have it. You will not ride to heaven on a featherbed; you must go on a pilgrimage. There is no going to the land of glory while you are sound asleep; dreamy sluggards will have to wake up in hell. If God has made you to feel in your soul the need of salvation, cry like one who is awake and alive. Be in earnest. Cry aloud. Spare not. And then I think you will find that my argument will be quite fair, that in all respects a reasonable, argumentative, intelligent prayer is more likely to prevail with God than the mere screaming, chattering noise of the raven, and that if he hears such a cry as the raven's, it is much more certain that he will hear yours.

Prayer Is More Congenial Than the Raven's Cry

All that the young ravens call for is food. Give them a little carrion, and they stop crying. Your cry must be much more pleasing to God's ear, for you entreat for forgiveness through the blood of his dear Son. It is a nobler occupation for the Most High to be bestowing spiritual gifts than natural gifts. The streams of grace flow from the upper springs. I know he is so condescending that he does not dishonor himself even when he drops food into the young raven's mouth, but still there is more honor about the work of giving peace, pardon, and reconciliation to the sons of men.

Eternal love appointed a way of mercy from before the foundation of the world, and infinite wisdom is engaged with boundless power to carry out the divine design. Surely the Lord must take much pleasure in saving the sons of men. If God is pleased to supply the beast of the field, do you not think he delights much more to supply his own child? I think you would find more congenial employment in teaching your own children than you would in merely foddering your ox or scattering barley among the fowls at the barn door, because there would be in the first work something nobler, which would more fully call up all your powers and bring out your inward self.

I am not left here to conjecture. It is written, "He delights in mercy." When God uses his power, he cannot be sad, for he is a happy God. But if there is such a thing possible as the Infinite Deity being happier at one time than at another, it is when he is forgiving sinners through the precious blood of Jesus.

Ah! sinner, when you cry to God, you give him an opportunity to do what he loves most to do, for he delights to forgive, to press his Ephraim to his bosom, to say of his prodigal son, "He was lost, but is found. He was dead but is alive again." This is more comfortable to the Father's heart than the feeding of the fatted calf or tending the cattle of a thousand hills.

Since then, dear friends, you are asking for something that will honor God far more to give than the mere gift of food to ravens, I think there comes a very forcible blow of my argumentative hammer tonight to break your unbelief in pieces. May God the Holy Spirit, the true Comforter, work in you mightily! Surely the God who gives food to ravens will not deny peace and pardon to seeking sinners. Try him! Try him at this moment! Indeed, stir not! Try him now.

The Ravens Are Not Commanded to Cry

We must not pause on any one point when the whole subject is so prolific. There is another source of comfort for you—namely, that *the ravens are nowhere commanded to cry.* When they cry, their petition is unwarranted by any specific exhortation from the divine mouth, but you have a warrant derived from divine exhortations to approach the throne of God in prayer.

If a rich man should open his house to those who were not invited, he would surely receive those who were invited. Ravens come without being invited to come, yet they are not sent away empty. You come invited as a guest—how may you be denied? Do you think you are not invited to come? Listen to this:

- "Everyone who calls on the name of the LORD will be saved." (Rom. 10:13)
- "Call upon me in the day of trouble; I will deliver you, and you shall glorify me." (Ps. 50:15)
- "Go into all the world and proclaim the gospel to the whole creation. Whoever believes and is baptized will be saved, but whoever does not believe will be condemned." (Mark 16:15–16)
- "Believe in the Lord Jesus Christ, and you will be saved." (Acts 16:31)
- "Repent and be baptized every one of you in the name of Jesus Christ." (Acts 2:38).

These are exhortations given without any limitation as to character. They freely invite you, indeed, they bid you come. Oh! after this can you think that God will spurn you? The window is open, the raven flies in, and the God of mercy does not chase it out. The door is open, and the word of promise bids you come—don't think that he will give you a denial, but believe rather that he will "receive you graciously, and love you freely," and then you will "render to him the calves of your lips." At any rate, try him! Try him even now!

Your Cry Is a Work of Grace

Again, there is yet another and a far mightier argument. The cry of a young raven is nothing but the natural cry of a creature, but your cry, if it is sincere, is the result of a work of grace in your heart.

When the raven cries to heaven, it is nothing but the raven's own self that cries. But when you cry, "God be merciful to me a sinner," it is God the Holy Spirit crying in you. It is the new life that God has given you, crying to the source from where it came to have further communion and communication with its great Original. It needs God himself to set a man praying in sincerity and in truth.

We can, if we think about it, teach our children to "say their prayers," but we cannot teach them to "pray." You may make a "prayer book," but you cannot put a grain of "prayer" into a book, for it is too spiritual a matter to be encased between pages. Some of you, perhaps, may "read prayers" in the family. I will not denounce the practice, but I will say this much of it: you may read those "prayers" for seventy years, and yet you may never once pray, for prayer is quite a different thing than mere words. True prayer is the trading of the heart with God, and the heart never comes into spiritual commerce with the ports of heaven until God the Holy Spirit puts wind into the sails and speeds the ship into its haven. "You must be born again." If there is any real prayer in your heart, though you may not know the secret, God the Holy Ghost is there.

Now if he hears cries that do not come from himself, how much more will he hear those that do! Perhaps you have been puzzling yourself to know whether your cry is a natural or a spiritual one. This may seem very important, and doubtless is so, but whether your cry is either the one or the other, still continue to seek the Lord. Possibly you doubt whether natural cries are heard by God. Let me assure you that they are.

I remember saying something on this subject on one occasion in a certain Ultra-Calvinistic place of worship. At that time, I was preaching to children and was exhorting them to pray, and I happened to say that long before any actual conversion, I had prayed for common mercies and that God had heard my prayers. This did not suit my good brethren of the superfine school, and afterward they all came around me professedly to know what I meant, but really to grumble and complain according to their nature and practice.

"They compassed me about like bees, yea, like bees they compassed me about!" After a while, as I expected, they fell to their usual amusement of calling names. They began to say what rank Arminianism this was, and another expression they were pleased to honor me with was the title of "Fullerism," a title, by the way, so honorable that I could heartily have thanked them for appending it to what I had advanced. But to say that God should hear the prayer of natural men was something worse than Arminianism to them, if indeed anything could be worse.

They quoted that counterfeit passage, "The prayer of the wicked is an abomination to the LORD," which I speedily answered by asking them if they would find me that text in the Word of God, for I ventured to assert that the devil was the author of that saying and that it was not in the Bible at all. "The sacrifice of the wicked is an abomination to the LORD" (Prov. 15:8) is in the Bible, but that is a very different thing from the "prayer of the wicked."

Moreover, there is a decided difference between the word *wicked* there intended and the natural man about whom we were arguing. I do not think that a man who begins to pray in any sense can be considered as being altogether among "the wicked" intended by Solomon, and certainly he is not among those who turn away their ear from hearing the law, of whom it is written that their prayer is an abomination. "Well, but" they said, "how could it be that God could hear a natural prayer?" And while I paused for a moment, an old woman in a red cloak pushed her way into the little circle round me, and said to them in a very forcible way, like a mother in Israel as she was, "Why do you raise this question, forgetting what God himself has said? What is this you say, that God does not hear natural prayer? Why, doesn't he hear the young ravens when they cry unto him, and do you think they offer spiritual prayers?" Straightway the men of war took to their heels. No defeat was more thorough, and for once in their lives, they must have felt that they might possibly err. Surely, brethren, this may encourage and comfort you.

I am not going to set you just now to the task of finding out whether your prayers are natural or spiritual, whether they come from God's Spirit or not, because that might, perhaps, discourage you. If the prayer proceeds from your very heart, we know how it got there, though you may not. God hears the ravens, and I do believe he will hear you, and I believe, moreover, though I do not now want to raise the question in your heart, that he hears your prayer, because, though you may not know it, there is a secret work of the Spirit of God going on within you that is teaching you to pray.

The Holy Spirit Aids Your Prayers

But I have mightier arguments and nearer the mark. When the young ravens cry, they cry alone, but when you pray, you have a mightier One than you praying with you.

Hear that sinner crying, "God, be merciful to me, a sinner" (Luke 18:13). Listen! Do you hear that other cry that goes up with his? No, you do not hear it because your ears are dull and heavy; but God hears it. There is another voice far louder and sweeter than the first and far more prevalent, mounting up at the same moment, and pleading, "Father, forgive them through my precious blood." The echo to the sinner's whisper is as majestic as the thunder's peal. There is never a sinner who truly prays without Christ praying at the same time. You cannot see nor hear him, but never does Jesus stir the depths of your soul by his Spirit without his soul being stirred too.

Oh, sinner! your prayer, when it comes before God, is a very different thing from what it is when it issues forth from you. Sometimes poor people come to us with petitions they wish to send to some company or great personage. They bring the petition and ask us to have it presented for them. It is very badly spelled, very strangely written, and we can just make out what they mean, but still, there is enough to let us know what they want.

First of all, we make out a fair copy for them, and then, having stated their case, we put our name at the bottom, and if we have any interest, of course, they get what they desire through the power of the name signed at the bottom of the petition. This is just what the Lord Jesus Christ does with our poor prayers. He makes a fair copy of them, stamps them with the seal of his own atoning blood, puts his own name at the bottom, and thus they go up to God's throne. It is your prayer, but oh! it is *his* prayer too. And it is the fact of it being his prayer that makes it prevail.

Now, this is a sledgehammer argument: if the ravens prevail when they cry all alone, if their poor chattering brings them what they want for themselves, how much more will the plaintive petitions of the poor trembling sinner prevail who can say, "For Jesus's sake," and who can clench all his own arguments with the blessed plea, "The Lord Jesus Christ deserves it. O Lord, give it to me for his sake."

I do trust that these seeking ones to whom I have been speaking, who have been crying so long and yet are afraid that they will never be heard, may not have to wait much longer but may soon have a gracious answer of peace, and if they will not just yet get the desire of their hearts, I hope they may be encouraged to persevere until the day of grace will dawn. You have a promise that the ravens have not, and that might make another argument if time permitted us to dwell on it. Trembler, having a promise to plead, never fear that you will not find success at the throne of grace!

And now, let me say to the sinner, in closing, *if you have cried unsuccessfully, still cry on.* "Go again seven times" indeeed, seventy times seven. Remember that the mercy of God in Christ Jesus is your only hope. Cling to it, then, as a drowning man clings to the only rope within reach. If you perish praying for mercy through the precious blood, you will be the first who ever perished so. Cry on. Just cry on, but oh! believe too, for believing brings the morning star and the day dawn.

When John Ryland's wife, Betty, lay dying, she was in great distress of mind, though she had been for many years a Christian. Her husband said to her in his quaint but wise way, "Well, Betty, what ails you?"

"Oh, John, I am dying, and I have no hope, John!"

"But, my dear, where are you going then?"

"I am going to hell!" was the answer.

"Well," he said, covering up his deep anguish with his usual humor, and meaning to strike a blow that would be sure to hit the nail on the head and put her doubts to speedy flight, "What do you intend doing when you get there, Betty?"

The good woman could give no answer, and Mr. Ryland continued, "Do you think you will pray when you get there?"

"Oh, John," she said, "I would pray anywhere. I cannot help praying."

"Well, then" he said, "they will say, 'Here is Betty Ryland, praying here in hell. Throw her out. We won't have anybody praying here. Throw her out.'"

This strange way of putting it brought light to her soul, and she saw at once the absurdity of the very suspicion of a soul really seeking Christ and yet being cast away forever from his presence.

Cry on, soul. Cry on! While the child can cry, it lives, and while you can besiege the throne of mercy, there is hope for you. But hear as well as cry, and believe what you hear, for it is by believing that peace is obtained.

But stay awhile, I have something else to say. Is it possible that you may have already obtained the very blessing you are crying after? "Oh," you say, "I would not ask for anything I had already received. If I knew I had it, I would stop crying and begin praising and blessing God." Now, I do not know whether all of you are in so safe a state, but I am persuaded that there are some seeking souls who have received the mercy for which they are asking. The Lord, instead of saying to them tonight, "Seek my face," is saying, "Why do you cry unto me? I have heard you in an acceptable hour, and in an acceptable time have I helped you. I have blotted out your sins like a cloud, and like a thick cloud, your iniquities. I have saved you. You are mine. I have cleansed you from all your sins. Go your way and rejoice." In such a case believing praise is more suitable than agonizing prayer.

"Oh," you say, "but it is not likely that I have the mercy while I am still seeking for it." Well, I don't know. Mercy sometimes falls down in a fainting fit outside the gate. Is it not possible for her to be taken inside while she is in the fainting fit, and for her to think all the while that she is still on the outside? She can hear the dog barking still, but ah, poor soul, when she comes to, she will find that she is inside the gate and is safe. So, some of you may happen to have fallen into a swoon of despondency just when you are coming to Christ. If so, may sovereign grace restore you, and perhaps I may be the means tonight of doing it.

What is it you are looking after? Some of you are expecting to see bright visions, but I hope you never may be gratified, for they are not worth a penny a thousand. All the visions in the world, since the days of miracles, put together, are but mere dreams after all, and dreams are nothing but vanity. People eat too much supper and then dream. It is indigestion or a morbid activity of the brain, and that is all. If that is all the evidence you have of conversion, you will do well to doubt it. I pray you never rest satisfied with it. It is wretched rubbish to build your eternal hopes on.

Perhaps you are looking for very strange feelings—not quite an electric shock but something very singular and peculiar. Believe me, you need never feel the strange motions you prize so highly. All those strange feelings some people speak of in connection with conversion may or may not be of any good to them, but I am certain they really have nothing to do with conversion so as to be at all necessary to it. I will put a question or two to you.

Do you believe yourself to be a sinner? "Yes," you say. But supposing I put that word *sinner* away? Do you mean that you believe you have broken God's law, that you are a good-for-nothing offender against God's government? Do you believe you have, in your heart, at any rate, broken all the commandments, and that you deserve punishment accordingly? "Yes," you say, "I not only believe that, but I feel it. It is a burden I carry about with me daily."

Now something more—do you believe that the Lord Jesus Christ can put all this sin of yours away? Yes, you do believe that. Then can you trust him to save you? You want saving. You cannot save yourself. Can you trust him to save you? "Yes," you say, "I already do that." Well, my dear friend, if you really trust Jesus, it is certain that you are saved, for you have the only evidence of salvation that is continual with any of us. There are other evidences that follow afterward, such as holiness and the graces of the Spirit, but the only evidence that is continual with the best of men living is this: *Simply to your cross, I cling.* Can you use Jack the huckster's verse?

> I'm a poor sinner and nothing at all,
> But Jesus Christ is my all in all.

I hope you will go a great deal further in experience on some points than this, but I do not want you to advance an inch further as to the ground of your evidence and the reason for your hope. Just stop there, and if now you look away from everything that is within you or without you to Jesus Christ, and trust in his sufferings on Calvary and in his whole atoning work as the ground of your acceptance before God, you are saved. You do not need anything more. You have passed from death to life. "He that believes on him is not condemned." "He that believes has everlasting life."

If I were to meet an angel presently in that aisle as I go out my door into my vestry, and he should say, "Charles Spurgeon, I have come from heaven to tell you that you are pardoned," I should say to him, "I know that without your telling me anything of the kind. I know it on a great deal better authority than yours." And if he asked me how I knew it, I would reply, "The word of God is better to me than the word of an angel, and he has said it, 'He that believes on him is not condemned.' I do believe on him, and therefore, I am not condemned, and I know it without an angel telling me so."

Do not, you troubled ones, be looking after angels and tokens and evidences and signs. If you rest on the finished work of Jesus, you have already the best evidence of your salvation in the world. You have God's word for it—what more is needed? Can you not take God's word? You can take your father's word. You can take your mother's word, why can you not take God's word? Oh! what vile hearts we must have to suspect God himself!

Perhaps you say you would not do such a thing. Oh! but you doubt God if you do not trust Christ for "whoever does not believe God has made him a liar" (1 John 5:10). If you do not trust Christ, you do in effect say that God is a liar. You do not want to say that, do you? Oh! believe the truthfulness of God! May the Spirit of God constrain you to believe the Father's mercy, the power of the Son's blood, and the willingness of the Holy Ghost to bring sinners to himself!

Come, my dear hearers, join with me in the prayer that you may be led by grace to see in Jesus all that you need.

> Prayer is a creature's strength, his very breath and being;
> Prayer is the golden key that can open the wicket of
>   mercy;
> Prayer is the magic sound that says to fate, So be it;
> Prayer is the slender nerve that moves the muscles of
>   Omnipotence,
> Wherefore, pray, O creature, for many and great are your
>   wants;
> Your mind, your conscience, and your being, your needs
>   commend you unto prayer,
> The cure of all cares, the grand panacea for all pains,
> Doubt's destroyer, ruin's remedy, the antidote to all
>   anxieties.

The Shameful Sufferer

No. 236, Music Hall, Royal Surrey Gardens,
London, England
January 30, 1859

*Who for the joy that was set before him endured the cross,
despising the shame, and is seated at the right
hand of the throne of God.
– Hebrews 12:2*

"Oh, what must I do, my Savior to praise?" Where will language be found that will describe his matchless, his unparalleled love toward the children of men? On any ordinary subject, one may find liberty of speech and fullness of utterance, but this subject lies out of the line of all oratory, and eloquence cannot attain unto it! This is one of the unutterable things—unutterable because it surpasses thought and defies the power of words.

How, then, can we deal with that which is unutterable? I am conscious that all I can say concerning the sufferings of Jesus this morning will be but as a drop in the bucket. None of us know the half of the agony he endured. None of us has ever fully comprehended the love of Christ that passes knowledge! Philosophers have probed the earth to its very center, threaded the spheres, measured the skies, weighed the hills—no, weighed the world itself—but this is one of those vast, boundless things which to measure surpasses all but the Infinite itself! As the swallow but skims the water and dives not into its depths, so all the descriptions of the preacher but skim the surface while depths immeasurable must lie far beneath our observation. Well might a poet say—

O love, you fathomless abyss!

For this love of Christ is indeed measureless and fathomless! None of us can attain unto it. In speaking of it, we feel our own weakness; we cast ourselves upon the strength of the Spirit, but even then, we feel that we can never attain unto the majesty of this subject. Before we can ever get a right idea of the love of Jesus, we must understand his previous glory in its height of majesty and his incarnation upon the earth in all its depths of shame.

Now, who can tell us the majesty of Christ? When he was enthroned in the highest heavens, he was very God of very God. By him were the heavens made and all the hosts thereof. By his power, he hung the earth upon nothing. His own almighty arm upheld the spheres—the pillars of the heavens rested on him. The praises of angels, archangels, cherubim, and seraphim perpetually surrounded him. The full chorus of the hallelujahs of the universe unceasingly flowed to the foot of his throne—he reigned supreme above all his creatures, God over all, blessed forever! Who can tell his height, then? And yet, this must be attained before we can measure the length of that mighty stoop he took when he came to earth to redeem our souls! And who, on the other hand, can tell how low he descended? To be a man was something, but to be a man of sorrows was far more. To bleed and die and suffer—these were much for him who was the Son of God! But to suffer as he did—such unparalleled agony. To endure as he did, a death of shame and a death by desertion of his God—this is a lower depth of condescending love even the most inspired mind must utterly fail to fathom! And yet, we must first understand infinite height and then infinite depth. We must measure, in fact, the whole infinite between heaven and hell before we can understand the love of Jesus Christ.

But because we cannot understand, will we therefore neglect? And because we cannot measure, will we therefore despise? Ah, no! Let us go to Calvary this morning and see this great sight—Jesus Christ, for the joy that was set before him, enduring the cross, despising the shame!

I will endeavor to show you, first, the *shameful sufferer;* secondly, I will endeavor to dwell on *his glorious motive;* and then thirdly, I will offer him to you as *an admirable example.*

The Shame of the Sufferer

Beloved, I wish to show you the *shameful sufferer.* The text speaks of shame, and therefore, before entering upon suffering, I will endeavor to say a word or two upon the shame.

Perhaps there is nothing men so much abhor as shame. We find that death itself has often been preferable in the minds of men to shame. And even the most wicked and callous-hearted have dreaded the shame and contempt of their fellow creatures far more than any tortures to which they could have been exposed. We find Abimelech, a man who murdered his own brethren without compunction—we find even him overcome by shame when "a certain woman threw an upper millstone on Abimelech's head and crushed his skull. Then he called quickly to the young man his armor-bearer and said to him, 'Draw your sword and kill me, lest they say of me, "A woman killed him."' And his young man thrust him through, and he died" (Judg. 9:53–54). Shame was too much for him! He would far rather meet the suicide's death—for such it was—than he should be convicted of the shame of being slain by a woman! So, it was with Saul—a man who was not ashamed of breaking his oath and of hunting his own son-in-law like a partridge on the mountains—even he fell upon his own sword rather than it should be said of him that he fell by the Philistines. And we read of an ancient king, Zedekiah, who albeit he seemed reckless enough, he was afraid to fall into the hands of the Chaldeans, lest the Jews who had fallen away to Nebuchadnezzar should mock him.

These instances are but a few of many. It is well known that criminals and malefactors have often had a greater fear of public contempt than of anything else. Nothing can so break down the human spirit as to continually be subject to contempt—the visible and manifest contempt of one's fellows! In fact, to go further, shame is so frightful to man that it is one of the ingredients of hell itself! It is one of the bitterest drops in that awful cup of misery— the shame of everlasting contempt to which wicked men awake in the day of their resurrection. To be despised of men, despised of angels, and despised of God is one of the depths of hell!

Shame, then, is a terrible thing to endure. And many of the proudest natures have been subdued when once they have been subjected to it. In the Savior's case, shame would be peculiarly shameful. The nobler a man's nature, the more readily does he perceive the slightest contempt and the more acutely does he feel it. That contempt that an ordinary man might bear without suffering—he who has been bred to be obeyed and who has all his life been honored—would feel most bitterly. Beggared princes and despised monarchs are among the most miserable of men! But here was our glorious Redeemer in whose face was the nobility of the Godhead itself, despised and spit upon and mocked! You may, therefore, wonder in amazement what such a noble nature as his had to endure! The mere kite can bear to be caged, but the eagle cannot bear to be hooded and blindfolded—he has a nobler spirit than that. The eyes that have faced the sun cannot endure darkness without a tear! But Christ who was more than noble—matchlessly noble, something more than of a royal race—for him to be shamed and mocked must have been dreadful, indeed!

Some minds are of such a delicate and sensitive disposition that they feel things far more than others. There are some of us who do not so readily perceive an affront, or when we do perceive it, we are totally indifferent to it. But there are others of a loving and tender heart. They have so long wept for others' woes that their hearts have become tender, and they therefore feel the slightest brush of ingratitude from those they love. If those for whom they are willing to suffer should utter words of blasphemy and rebuke against them, their souls would be pierced to the very quick! A man in armor would walk through thorns and briars without feeling, but a man who is naked feels the smallest of the thorns. Now Christ was, so to speak, a naked spirit. He had stripped himself of all for mankind. He said, "The foxes have holes and the birds of the air have nests, but the Son of Man has nowhere to lay his head." He stripped himself of everything that could make him callous, for he loved with all his soul. His strong passionate heart was fixed upon the welfare of the human race! He loved them even unto death. And to be mocked by those for whom he died, to be spit on by the creatures he came to save, to come to his own and to find that his own would not receive him but actually cast him out, this was pain, indeed! You tender hearts can weep for others' woes, and you who love with a love as strong as death and with a jealousy as cruel as the grave—you can guess, but only guess—what the Savior must have endured when all did mock him, all did scorn him, and he found none to pity—none to take his part.

To go back to the point with which we started, shame is peculiarly abhorrent to humanity, and far more to such humanity as that which Christ carried about with him—a noble, sensitive, loving nature such as no other person had ever possessed!

And now come and let us behold the pitiful spectacle of Jesus put to shame. He was put to shame in three ways—by shameful accusation, shameful mockery, and shameful crucifixion.

And first, behold the Savior's shame in his shameful accusation. He in whom was no sin and who had done no ill was charged with sin of the blackest kind! He was first arraigned before the Sanhedrin on no less a charge than that of blasphemy. And could he blaspheme? Could he who said, "My food is to do the will of him who sent me," blaspheme? He who in the depths of his agony when he sweat, as it were, great drops of blood, at last cried, "Father, if you are willing, remove this cup from me. Nevertheless, not my will, but yours, be done"—could he blaspheme? No! And it is just because it was so contrary to his character that he felt the accusation. To charge some of you here present with having blasphemed God would not startle you, for you have done it and have done it so often as almost to forget that God abhors blasphemers, and that he "will not hold him guiltless who takes his name in vain." But for one who loved as Jesus loved and obeyed as he obeyed—for him to be charged with *blasphemy*—the accusation must have caused him peculiar suffering! We wonder that he did not fall to the ground, even as his betrayers did when they came to lay hold of him! Such an accusation as that might blight an angel's spirit. Such a slander might wither the courage of a cherub. Do not marvel, then, that Jesus felt the shame of being accused of such a crime as this!

Nor did this satisfy them. Having charged him with breaking the first table, they then charged him with violating the second—they said he was guilty of sedition. They declared that he was a traitor to the government of Caesar, that he stirred up the people, declaring that he himself was a king. And could he commit treason? He who said, "My kingdom is not of this world, else would my servants fight." He who, when they would have taken him by force to make him a king, withdrew himself into the wilderness and prayed—could he commit treason? It would be impossible! Did he not pay tribute and sent for the fish when his poverty had not the means to pay the tax? Could he commit treason? He could not sin against Caesar, for he was Caesar's Lord! He was King of kings and Lord of lords! If he had chosen to, he could have taken the purple from the shoulders of Caesar and, at a word, have given Caesar to be a prey to the worms! Jesus Christ commit treason? It was far enough from Jesus, the gentle and the mild, to stir up sedition or set man against man. Ah no, he was a lover of his country and a lover of his race! He would never provoke a civil war, and yet this charge was brought against him. What would you think, good citizens and good Christians, if you were charged with such a crime as this—with the clamors of your own people behind you, crying out against you, as so dreadful an offender that you must die? Would not that abash you? Ah, but your Master had to endure this as well as the other! He despised the shameful indictments and was numbered with the transgressors!

But next, Christ not only endured shameful accusation but also *shameful mocking*. When Christ was taken away to Herod, Herod "set him at nought." The original word means "made nothing" of him. It is an amazing thing to find that man should make nothing of the Son of God who is all-in-all. Jesus had made himself nothing. He had declared that he was a worm and no man. But what a sin that was, and what a shame that was, when Herod made him nothing! He had but to look Herod in the face and he could have withered him with one glance of his fire-darting eyes! But yet Herod may mock him, Jesus will not speak, and men of arms may come about him and break their cruel jests upon his tender heart, but not a word has he to say, but "like a lamb that is led to the slaughter, and like a sheep before its shearers is silent, so he opened not his mouth."

You will observe that in Christ's mocking, from Herod's own hall on to the time when he was taken from Pilate's hall of judgment to his crucifixion, and then onward to his death, the mocking were of many kinds. In the first place, they mocked the Savior's person. One of those things about which we may say very little but of which we should often think on is the fact that our Savior was stripped, amid a vulgar soldiery, of all his garments. It is a shame even for us to speak of this that was done by our own flesh and blood toward him who is our Redeemer! Those holy limbs that were the casket of the precious jewel of his soul were exposed to the shame and open contempt of men—coarse-minded men who were utterly destitute of every particle of delicacy! The person of Christ was stripped twice. And although our painters, for obvious reasons, cover Christ upon the cross [when they depict him], there he hung—the naked Savior of a naked race! He who clothed the lilies had nothing with which to clothe himself! He who had clothed the earth with jewels and made for it robes of emeralds had not so much as a rag to conceal his nakedness from a staring, gazing, mocking, hardhearted crowd! He had made coats of skins for Adam and Eve when they were naked in the garden. He had taken from them those poor fig leaves with which they sought to hide their nakedness, given them something with which they might wrap themselves from the cold. But now, they divided his garments among them, and for his robe they cast lots, while he himself, exposed to the pitiless storm of contempt, had no cloak with which to cover his shame! They mocked his person—Jesus Christ declared himself to be the Son of God—they mocked his *divine person* as well as his human—when he hung upon the cross, they said, "If you are the Son of God, come down from the cross, and we will believe on you." Frequently they challenged him to prove his divinity by turning aside from the work that he had undertaken. They asked him to do the very things that would have disproved his divinity in order that they might then—as they declared—acknowledge and confess that he was the Son of God!

And now, can you think of it? Christ was mocked as man—we can conceive him as yielding to this—but to be mocked as *God!* A challenge thrown to manhood, manhood would easily take up and fight the duel. Christian manhood would allow the gauntlet to lie there, or tread it beneath its feet in contempt, bearing all things and enduring all things for Christ's sake. But can you think of God being challenged by his creature—the eternal Jehovah provoked by the creature his own hand has made? The Infinite despised by the finite? He who fills all things—by whom all things *exist*—laughed at, mocked, despised by the creature of an hour, who is crushed before the moth! This was contempt, indeed, a contempt of his complex person, of his manhood and of his divinity!

But note next they mocked all his offices as well as his person. Christ was a king and never such a king as he. He is Israel's David. All the hearts of his people are knit unto him. He is Israel's Solomon. He will reign from sea to sea and from the river even to the ends of the earth! He was one of royal race! We have some called kings on earth, children of Nimrod—these are called kings, but kings they are not. They borrow their dignity of him who is King of kings and Lord of lords. But here was one of the true blood, one of the right royal race who had lost his way and was mingled with the common herd of men! What did they do? Did they bring crowns with which to honor him, and did the nobility of earth cast their robes beneath his feet to carpet his footsteps? No! He is delivered up to rough and brutal soldiers. They find for him a mimic throne, and having put him on it, they strip him of his own robes and find some old soldier's cloak of scarlet or of purple and put it about his loins. They plait a crown of thorns and put it about his brow—a brow that was of old benighted with stars! And then they fix in his hand—a hand that will not resent an insult—a reed scepter! Then bowing the knee, they pay their mimic homage before him, making him a May-day king.

Now, perhaps there is nothing so heartrending as despised royalty! You have read the story of an English king who was taken out by his cruel enemies to a ditch. They seated him on an anthill, telling him that was his throne, and then they washed his face in the filthiest puddle they could find. And with tears running down his cheeks, he said, "I shall yet be washed in clean water," though he was bitterly mistaken. But think of the King of kings and Lord of lords having for his adoration the spit of guilty mouths, for homage the smiting of filthy hands, for tribute the jests of brutal tongues! Was ever shame like yours, you King of kings, you emperor of all worlds flouted by the soldiers and smitten by their menial hands? O earth! How could you endure this iniquity? O you heavens! Why did you not fall in very indignation to crush the men who thus blasphemed your Maker? Here was a shame, indeed—the King mocked by his own subjects!

He was a prophet, too, as we all know, and what did they do that they might mock him as a prophet? Why, they blindfolded him—shut out the light of heaven from his eyes and then they struck him and buffeted him with their hands and said, "Prophecy to us who it is that struck you." The prophet must make a prophecy to those who taunted him, to tell them who it was who struck him! We love prophets. It is but the nature of mankind that if we believe in a prophet, we should love him. We believe that Jesus was the first and the last of prophets. By him all others were sent. We bow before him with reverential adoration. We count it to be our highest honor to sit at his feet like Mary. We only wish that we might have the comfort to wash his feet with our tears and wipe them with the hairs of our head. We feel that, like John the Baptist, his shoelaces we are not worthy to loosen, and can we, therefore, bear the spectacle of Jesus the prophet blindfolded and buffeted with insult and blows?

But they also mocked his priesthood! Jesus Christ had come into the world to be a priest to offer sacrifice, and his priesthood must be mocked, too! All salvation lay in the hands of this priest, and now they say to him, "If you are the Christ, save yourself and us!" "Ah, he saved others; he could not save himself," they laughed! But oh, what mystery of scorn is here! What unutterable depths of shame that the great High Priest of our profession—he who is the Passover Lamb, the altar, the priest, the sacrifice—that he, the Son of God incarnate, the Lamb of God who takes away the sins of the world, should thus be despised and thus be mocked!

He was mocked, still further, *in his sufferings.* I cannot venture to describe the sufferings of our Savior under the lash of the scourge. Saint Bernard and many of the early fathers of the church gave such a picture of Christ's scourging that I could not endure to tell it again! Whether they had sufficient data for what they said, I do not know. But this much I know—"He was pierced for our transgressions; he was crushed for our iniquities; upon him was the chastisement that brought us peace, and with his wounds we are healed" (Isa. 53:5). I know it must have been a terrible scourging to be called *pierced, crushed, chastisement,* and *wounds.*

And remember, every time the lash fell on his shoulders, the laugh of him who used the lash was mingled with the stripe—and every time the blood poured out afresh, and the flesh was torn off his bones, there was a jest and a jeer to make his pain yet more poignant and terrible! And when he came at last to his cross and they nailed him on it, how they continued the mockery of his sufferings! We are told that the high priests and the scribes stood, and at length sat and watched him there. When they saw his head fall upon his breast, they would, no doubt, make some bitter remark about it and say, "Ah, he will never lift his head again among the multitude." And when they saw his hands bleeding, they would say, "Ha, ha, these were the hands that touched the lepers, and that raised the dead—they will never do that again!" And when they saw his feet, they would say, "Ah, those feet will never tread this land again and journey on his pilgrimages of mercy." And then some course, some villainous, some brutal, perhaps some beastly jest would be made concerning every part of his thrice-adorable person! They mocked him, and at last he called for a drink, and they gave him vinegar—mocking his thirst while they pretended to relieve it!

But worst of all, I have one more thing to notice—they mocked *his prayers*. Did you ever read in all the annals of executions or of murders that ever men mocked their fellow-creatures' *prayers?* I have read stories of some dastardly villains who have sought to slay their enemies, and seeing their death approaching, the victims have said, "Give me a moment or two for prayer"— and rare has been the cases when this has been disallowed! But I never read of a case in which, when the prayer was uttered, it has been laughed at and made the object of a jest! But here hangs the Savior, and every word he speaks becomes the subject of a pun, the motto of a jest. And when at the last he utters the most thrilling death-shriek that ever startled earth and hell, "*Eloi, Eloi, lama Sabacthani*," even then they must pun upon it and say, "He calls for Elijah; let us see whether Elijah will come and take him down." He was mocked even in his prayer! O Jesus! Never was love like yours; never patience that could be compared with your endurance, when you endured the cross, despising the shame!

I feel that in thus describing the Savior's mockeries, I have not been able to set before you the fullness of the shame through which he passed and will have to attempt it yet again, in another moment, when I come to describe *his shameful death*, taking the words that preceded the ones I have already enlarged upon. He endured the cross just as he despised the shame.

The cross! The cross! When you hear that word, it wakens in your hearts no thoughts of shame. There are other forms of capital punishment in the present day far more disgraceful than the cross. Connected with the guillotine, there is much humiliation with the block, as much with the gallows, most of all.

But, remember, that although to speak of the gallows is to utter a word of disgrace, yet there is nothing of shame in the term *gallows* compared with the shame of the cross as it was understood in the days of Christ! We are told that crucifixion was a punishment to which none could be put but a slave. Even then, the crime must have been of the most frightful character—such as the betrayal of a master, the plotting his death or murdering him—only such offenses would have brought crucifixion, even, upon a slave. It was looked upon as the most terrible and frightful of all punishments. All the deaths in the world are preferable to this! They have all some slight alleviating circumstance—either their quickness or their glory. But this is the death of a villain, of a murderer, of an assassin—a death painfully protracted—one that cannot be equaled in all inventions of human cruelty for suffering and humiliation! Christ himself endured this. The cross, I say, is in this day no theme of shame. It has been the crest of many a monarch—the banner of many a conqueror! To some it is an object of adoration. The finest engravings and the most wonderful paintings have been dedicated to this subject. And now the cross engraved on many a gem has become a right royal and noble thing. But we are unable at this day, I believe, to fully understand the shame of the cross. But the Jew knew it. The Roman knew it. And Christ knew what a frightful thing, what a shameful thing, it was to be put to the death of crucifixion.

Remember, too, that in the Savior's case, there were special aggravations of this shame. He had to carry his own cross. He was crucified, too, at the common place of execution—Calvary, analogous to our ancient Tyburn or our present Old Bailey. He was put to death, too, at a time when Jerusalem was full of people. It was at the feast of the Passover, when the crowd had greatly increased and when the representatives of all nations would be present to behold the spectacle. Parehians, Medes, Elamites, and the dwellers in Mesopotamia, in Greece, yes, and perhaps far-off Tarshish and the islands of the sea—all were there to unite in this scoffing and to increase the shame! And he was crucified between two thieves, as if to teach that he was viler than they! Was there ever shame like this?

Let me conduct you to the cross. The cross, the cross! Tears begin to flow at the very thought of it. The rough wood is laid on the ground. Christ is flung on his back. Four soldiers seize his hands and feet! His blessed flesh is rent with the accursed iron. He begins to bleed. He is lifted into mid-air—the cross is dashed into the place prepared for it—every limb of my Savior is dislocated—every bone put out of joint by that terrific jerk! He hangs there naked to his shame, gazed upon by all beholders! The sun shines hot upon him; fever begins to burn; his tongue is dried up like a potsherd—it cleaves to the roof of his mouth—he has nothing with which to nourish his mouth with moisture. His body has been long emaciated by fasting. He has been brought near the brink of death by flagellation in the hall of Pilate. There he hangs. The tenderest pares of his body—his hands and feet—are pierced, and where the nerves are most numerous and tender, there is the iron rending and tearing its fearful way! The weight of his body drags the iron up his feet; his knees are so weary they cannot hold him, and then the iron begins to drag through his hands! Terrible spectacle, indeed!

But you have seen only the outward—there was an inward. You cannot see that—if you could see it, though your eyes were like the angels, you would be struck with eternal blindness! Then there was the soul. The soul dying! Can you guess what must be the pangs of a soul dying? A soul never died on earth yet. Hell is the place of dying souls, where they die everlastingly the second death. And there was within the ribs of Christ's body, hell itself poured out! Christ's soul was enduring the conflict with all the powers of hell, whose malice was aggravated by the fact that it was the last battle they should ever be able to fight with him! No, worse than that—he had lost that which is the martyr's strength and shield—he had lost the presence of his God! God himself was putting his hand upon him! It pleased the Father to crush him! He had put him to grief; he had made his soul a sacrifice for sin! God, in whose countenance Christ had everlastingly seemed himself, basking in delight, concealed his face! And there was Jesus forsaken of God and man, left alone to tread the winepress—no, to be *trod in the winepress*—and dip his clothes in his own blood! Oh, was there ever grief like this? No love can picture it! If I had a thought in my heart concerning the suffering of Christ, it would chafe my lips before I uttered it! The agonies of Jesus were like the furnace of Nebuchadnezzar, heated seven times hotter than any human suffering was heated before. Every vein was a road for the hot feet of pain to travel in—every nerve a string in a harp of agony that was thrilled with the discordant wail of hell! All the agonies that the damned themselves can endure were thrust into the soul of Christ! He was a target for the arrows of the Almighty—arrows dipped in the poison of our sin! All the billows of the Eternal dashed upon this rock of our salvation! He must be bruised, trod, crushed, destroyed—his soul must be exceedingly sorrowful, even to death.

But I must pause; I cannot describe it. I can creep over it, and you can too. The rocks split in two when Jesus died! Our hearts must be made of harder marble than the rocks themselves if they do not feel! The temple tore its gorgeous veil of tapestry, and will not you be mourners too? The sun itself had one big tear in its burning eye, which quenched its light. And will we not weep? We for whom the Savior died? Will we not feel an agony of heart that he should thus have endured for us?

Mark, my friends, that all the shame that came on Christ, he despised! He counted it so light, compared with the joy that was set before him, that he is said to have despised it! As for his sufferings, he could not despise them—that word could not be used in connection with the cross, for the cross was too awful for even Christ himself to despise! That, he *endured*. The shame he could cast off, but the cross he must carry, and to it, he must be nailed. "He endured the cross, despising the shame."

His Glorious Motive

What was that which made Jesus speak like this? It was "for the joy that was set before him." Beloved, what was the joy? Oh, what a thought that must melt a rock and make a heart of iron move! The joy that was set before Jesus was principally the joy of saving you and me! I know it was the joy of fulfilling his

Father's will—of sitting down on his Father's throne—of being made perfect through suffering—but still, I know this is the grand, great motive of the Savior's suffering—the joy of saving *us!* Do you know what the joy is of doing good to others? If you do not, I pity you, for of all joys God has left in this poor wilderness, this is one of the sweetest! Have you seen the hungry when they have needed bread for many an hour—have you seen them come to your house almost naked—their clothes having been thrust away, that they might get money to buy bread? Have you heard the woman's story of the griefs of her husband? Have you listened when you have heard the tale of imprisonment, of sickness, of cold or hunger, of thirst, and have you never said, "I will clothe you; I will feed you"? Have you never felt that divine joy when your gold has been given to the poor and your silver has been dedicated to the Lord; when you bestowed it upon the hungry and you have gone aside and said, "God forbid that I should be self-righteous—but I do feel it is worth living for—to feed the hungry and clothe the naked, and to do good to my poor suffering fellow creatures"? Now, this is the joy Christ felt! It was the joy of feeding us with the bread of heaven—the joy of clothing poor, naked sinners in his own righteousness—the joy of finding mansions in heaven for homeless souls—of delivering us from the prison of hell and giving us the eternal enjoyments of heaven!

But why should Christ look on us? Why should he choose to do this for us? Oh, my friends, we never deserved anything at his hands! As a good old writer says, "When I look at the crucifixion of Christ, I remember that *my* sins put him to death. I see not Pilate, but I see myself in Pilate's place, bearing Christ for honor. I hear not the cry of the Jews, but I hear my sins yelling out, 'Crucify him! Crucify him!' I see not iron nails, but I see my own iniquities fastening him to the cross! I see no spear, but I behold my unbelief piercing his poor wounded side—

For You, my sins, my cruel sins, his chief tormentors were!
Each of my sins became a nail and unbelief the spear.

It is the opinion of the Romanist that the very man who pierced Christ's side was afterward converted and became a follower of Jesus. I do not know whether that is *the* fact, but I know it is the case *spiritually*. I know that *we* have pierced the Savior. I know that *we* have crucified him. And yet, strange to say, the blood that we fetched from those holy veins has washed us from our sins and has made us accepted in the beloved! Can you understand this? Here is mankind, mocking the Savior, parading him through the streets, nailing him to a cross, and then sitting down to mock at his agonies. And yet, what is there in the heart of Jesus but love to them? He is weeping all this, while they would crucify him—not so much because he felt the suffering, though that was much, but because he could not bear the thought that men whom he loved could nail him to the tree! "That was the unkindest stab of all."

You remember that remarkable story of Julius Caesar when he was struck by his friend Brutus. "When the noble Caesar saw him stab, ingratitude stronger than traitor's arms quite vanquished him! Then burst his mighty heart." Now Jesus had to endure the stab in his inmost heart, and to know that his *elect* did it—that his *redeemed* did it, that his own church was his murderer—that his own people nailed him to the tree! Can you think, beloved, how strong must have been the love that made him submit even to this?

Picture yourself today going home from this hall. You have an enemy who all his life long has been your enemy. His father was your enemy, and he is your enemy too. Never a day passes but you try to win his friendship. But he spits on your kindness and curses your name. He does injury to your friends, and there is not a stone he leaves unturned to do you damage. As you are going home, today, you see a house on fire. The flames are raging, and the smoke is ascending in one black column to heaven. Crowds gather in the street, and you are told there is a man in the upper chamber who will be burned to death. No one can save him! You say, "Why, that is my enemy's house." And you see him at the window. It is your own enemy—the very man! He is about to be burned alive. Full of lovingkindness, you say, "I will save that man if I can." He sees you approach the house. He puts his head out the window and curses you! "An everlasting blast upon you!" he says. "I would rather perish than that you should save me."

Can you imagine yourself, then, dashing through the smoke and climbing the blazing staircase to save him? And can you conceive that when you get near him, he struggles with you and tries to roll you in the flames? Can you conceive your love to be so potent that you can perish in the flames rather than leave him to be burned? You say, "I could not do it. It is above flesh and blood to do it!" But Jesus did it! We hated him; we despised him, and when he came to save us, we rejected him! When his Holy Spirit comes into our hearts to strive with us, we resist him! But he will save us—no, he himself braved the fire that he might snatch us as brands from eternal burning! The joy of Jesus was the joy of saving sinners. The great motive, then, with Christ in enduring all this was that he might save us!

Our Imitation

I speak now to Christians—to those who have tasted and handled of the good word of life. Christian men and women! If Christ endured all this merely for the joy of saving *you*, will you be ashamed of bearing *anything* for Christ? The words are on my lips again this morning—

> If on my face for your dear name,
>   shame and reproach shall be,
> I'll hail reproach and welcome shame,
>   my Lord, I'll die for thee.

Oh, I do not wonder that the martyrs died for such a Christ as this! When the love of Christ is shed abroad in our hearts, then we feel that if the stake were present, we would stand firmly in the fire to suffer for him who died for us! I know our poor unbelieving hearts would soon begin to quail at the crackling wood and the furious heat, but surely this love would prevail over all our unbelief—are there any of you who feel that if you follow Christ, you must lose by it, lose your station or lose your reputation?

Will you be laughed at if you leave the world and follow Jesus? Oh, and will you turn aside because of these little things, when he would not turn aside though all the world mocked him until he could say, "It is finished"? No, by the grace of God, let every Christian lift his hands to the Most High God, to the maker of heaven and earth, and let him say within himself—

> Now for the love I bear his name,
> what was my gain I count my loss!
> I pour contempt on all my shame,
> and nail my glory to his cross.

"For me to live is Christ; to die is gain." Living I will be his; dying I will be his. I will live to his honor; serve him wholly, if he will help me—and if he needs it—I will die for his name's sake![1]

---

1 Spurgeon was so carried away with the first head that he was unable, from lack of time, to touch on the other points. May what was blessed to the hearer be sweet to the reader.

The Soul Winner

**No. 1292, Metropolitan Tabernacle,
Newington, London, England,
January 20, 1876**

*The fruit of the righteous is a tree of life,
and he who wins souls is wise.*
– Proverbs 11:30 (NKJV)

I had very great joy last night—many of you know why, but some do not. We held our annual meeting of the church, and it was a very pleasant sight to see so many brothers and sisters knit together in the heartiest love, welded together as one mass by common sympathies, and holding firmly to "one Lord, one faith, and one baptism." Think of a church with 4,900 members! Such a community has seldom been gathered in any age, and in the present century it is without parallel. "O Lord, You have multiplied the people, and increased the joy. They joy before You as the joy of harvest." It brings tears into one's eyes to look upon so many who declare themselves to be members of the body of Christ. The hope that so many are plucked as brands from the burning and delivered from the wrath to come is in itself exceedingly consoling, and I felt the joy of it while communing with my brothers and sisters in Christ Jesus.

On thinking it over afterward, however, it seemed to me that there is a higher joy in looking at a body of believers than that which arises from merely regarding them as saved. There is a great joy in salvation, a joy worthy to stir the angelic harps. Think of the Savior's agony in the ransom of every one of his redeemed. Think of the work of the Holy Spirit in every renewed heart. Think of the love of the Father as resting on every one of the regenerates. I could not, if I took up my parable for a month, set forth all the mass of joy that is to be seen in a multitude of believers, if we only look at what God has done *for* them, promised *to* them, and will fulfill *in* them!

But there is yet a wider field of thought, and my mind has been thinking about it all day—the thought of the capacities of *service* contained in a numerous band of believers, the possibilities of blessing *others* that lie within the bosoms of regenerate persons. We must not think so much of what we already are as to forget what the Lord may accomplish by us for others! Here are the coals of fire, but who will describe the conflagration that they may cause?

We ought to regard the Christian church not as a luxurious hotel where Christians may each one dwell at his ease, in his own suite, but as a *barracks* in which soldiers are gathered together to be drilled and trained for war. We should regard the Christian church not as an association for mutual admiration and comfort but as an arm with banners, marching to the fray to achieve victories for Christ, to storm the strongholds of the enemy, and to add province after province to the Redeemer's kingdom! We may view converted persons when gathered into church membership as so much wheat in the granary, and we thank God that it is there, and that so far, the harvest has rewarded the sower, but far more soul-inspiring is the view when we regard those believers as each one likely to be made a living center for the extension of the kingdom of Jesus! Then we see them sowing the fertile valleys of our land and promising before long to bring forth some thirty, some forty, some fifty, and some a hundredfold! The capacities of life are enormous—one becomes a thousand in a marvelously brief space; within a short time, a few grains of wheat would suffice to seed the whole world, and a few true saints might suffice for the conversion of all nations! Only take that which comes from one ear, store it well, sow it all—again store it next year, and then sow it all again—and the multiplication almost exceeds the power of computation! Oh, that every Christian was thus year by year the Lord's seed corn! If all the wheat in the world had perished except a single grain, it would not take many years to replenish all the earth and sow its fields and plains. But in a far shorter time, in the power of the Holy Spirit, one Paul or one Peter would have evangelized all lands! View yourselves as grains of wheat predestinated to seed the world! That man lives grandly who is as earnest as if the very existence of Christianity depended on him and is determined that to all men within his reach will be made known the unsearchable riches of Christ.

If we whom Christ is pleased to use as his seed corn were only all scattered and sown as we ought to be and were all to sprout and bring forth the green blade and the corn in the ear, what a harvest there would be! Again would it be fulfilled, "There will be an abundance of grain in the earth, on the top of the mountains"—a very bad position for it—"Its fruit shall wave like Lebanon; and those of the city shall flourish like grass of the earth" (Ps. 72:16 NKJV). May God grant us to feel tonight some degree of the Holy Spirit's quickening power while we talk together, not so much about what God has done for us as about what God may do *by* us and how far we may put ourselves into a right position to be used by him.

There are two things in the text found laid out with much distinctness in its two sentences. The first is this: *the life of the believer is, or ought to be, full of soul-blessing*—"The fruit of the righteous is a tree of life." In the second place, *the pursuit of the believer ought always to be soul-winning.* The second is much the same as the first, only the first head sets forth our unconscious influence, and the second, our efforts we put forth with the avowed objective of winning souls for Christ.

1. Let us begin at the beginning, because the second cannot be carried out without the first; without fullness of life within,

there cannot be an overflow of life to others. It is of no use for any of you to try to be soul-winners if you are not bearing fruit in your own lives. How can you serve the Lord with your lips if you do not serve him with your lives? How can you preach with your tongues his gospel when with hands, feet, and hearts you are preaching the devil's gospel and setting up antichrist by your practical unholiness? We must first have life and bear personal fruit to the divine glory, and then out of our example will spring the conversion of others! Let us go to the fountainhead and see how the man's own life is essential to his being useful to others.

The Life of the Believer Is Full of Blessings

This fact, we will consider by means of a few observations growing out of the text, and first let us remark that *the believer's outward life comes as a matter of fruit from him*. This is important to notice. The fruit of the righteous—that is to say, his *life*—is not a thing fastened *upon* him; it grows *out* of him. It is not a garment he puts off and on, but it is inseparable from himself. The sincere man's religion is the *man* himself and not a cloak for his concealment. True godliness is the natural outgrowth of a renewed nature; the forced does not grow of joyous excitement. Is it not natural for a vine to bear clusters of grapes? Is it not natural for a palm tree to bear dates? Certainly, as natural as it is for the apples of Sodom to be found on the trees of Sodom, and for noxious plants to produce poisonous berries, when God gives a new nature to his people, the lily that comes out of that new nature springs spontaneously from it. The man who has a religion that is not part and parcel of himself will by-and-by discover that it is worse than useless to him. The man who wears his piety like a mask at a carnival so that when he gets home he changes from a saint to a savage, from an angel to a devil, from John to Judas, from a benefactor to a bully—such a man, I say, knows very well what formalism and hypocrisy can do for him, and he has no vestige of true religion. Fig trees do not bear figs on certain days and thorns at other times, but they are true to their nature at all seasons. Those who think that godliness is a matter of vestment and have an intimate relationship with blue and scarlet and fine linen are consistent if they keep their religion to the proper time for the wearing of their sacred pomposities. But he who has discovered what Christianity is knows that it is much more a *life* than an act, a form, or a profession. Much as I love the creed of Christendom, I am ready to say that true Christianity is far more a life than a creed. It is a creed, and it has its ceremonies, but it is mainly a *life*—it is a divine spark of heaven's own flame that falls into the human bosom and burns within, consuming much that lies hidden in the soul, and then, at last, as a heavenly life, flaming forth, so as to be seen and felt by those around.

Under the indwelling power of the Holy Spirit, a regenerate person becomes like that bush in Horeb that was all aglow with Deity. The God within him makes him shine so that the place around him is holy ground, and those who look at him feel the power of his hallowed life. Dear brothers and sisters, we must take care that our religion is more and more a matter of outgrowth from our souls. Many professors are hedged about with "You must not do this or that" and are driven onward with "You must do this, and you must do that." But there is a doctrine, too often perverted, that is, nevertheless, a blessed truth of God and ought to dwell in your hearts. "You are not under the law but under grace"; therefore, you do not obey the will of God because you hope to earn heaven or dream of escaping from divine wrath by your works but because there is a life in you that seeks after that which is holy, pure, right, and true and cannot endure that which is evil. You are careful to maintain good works, not from either legal hopes or legal fears but because there is a holy thing within you, born of God, that seeks, according to its nature, to do that which is pleasing to God. Look to it more and more so that your religion is real, true, natural, and vital—not artificial, constrained, or superficial. We all need a religion that can live either in a wilderness or in a crowd. We need a religion that will show itself in every walk of life and in every company. Give me the godliness, which is seen at home, especially around the fireside, for it is never more beautiful than there! Give me the godliness that is seen in the battle and tussle of ordinary business among scoffers and gainsayers as well as among Christian men.

Show me the faith that can defy the lynx eyes of the world and walk fearlessly where all scowl with the fierce eyes of hate or where there are no observers to sympathize and no friends to judge leniently! May you be filled with the life of the Spirit, and your whole conduct and conversation be the natural and blessed outgrowth of that Spirit's indwelling!

Note next that *the fruit which comes from a Christian is fruit worthy of his character.* "The fruit of the righteous is a tree of life." Each tree bears its own fruit and is known by it. The righteous man bears righteous fruit—and do not let us be at all deceived, brothers and sisters, or fall into any error about this—"whoever practices righteousness is righteous" (1 John 3:7) and "whoever does not practice righteousness is not of God, nor is the one who does not love his brother" (3:10). We are prepared, I hope, to die for the doctrine of justification by faith, and to assert before all adversaries that salvation is not of works. But we also confess that we are justified by a faith that *produces* works, and if any man has a faith that does not produce good works, it is the faith of devils! Saving faith appropriates the finished work of the Lord Jesus, and so saves by itself alone, for we are justified by faith without works—but the faith that is without works cannot bring salvation to any man! We are saved by faith without works, but not by a faith that is without works, for the real faith that saves the soul works by Christ's love and purifies the character. If you can cheat across the counter, your hope of heaven is a cheat too; though you can pray as prettily as anybody and practice acts of outward piety as well as any other hypocrite, you are deceived if you expect to be right at last! If as a lazy employee lying and loitering, or if as an employer you are hard, tyrannical, and unchristian-like toward your employees, your fruit shows that you are a tree of Satan's own orchard and bear apples that will suit *his* tooth! If you can practice tricks of the trade, and if you can lie—and how many do lie every day about their neighbors or their goods?—you may talk about being justified by faith all you like, but all liars will have their portion in the lake that burns with fire and brimstone! And among the biggest liars you will be, for you are guilty of the lie of saying, "I am a Christian," whereas you are not! A false profession is one of the worst of lies since it brings the utmost dishonor upon Christ and his people. The fruit of the righteous is righteousness—the fig tree will not bring forth thorns; neither will we gather grapes from thistles. A tree is known by its fruit, but we cannot judge men's hearts, and must not try to do so. We *can* judge their lives, and I pray God we may all be ready to judge our own lives and see if we are bringing forth righteous fruit, for if not, we are not righteous!

Let it, however, never be forgotten that the fruit of the righteous, though it comes from him naturally—for his newborn nature yields the sweet fruit of obedience—yet it is always the result of grace, which is the gift of God! There is no truth of God that ought to be remembered more than this: "From me comes your fruit" (Hos. 14:8). We can bring forth no fruit except as we abide in Christ! The righteous will flourish as a branch, and only as a branch! How does a branch flourish? By its connection with the stem and the consequent flowing in of the sap, and so, though the righteous man's righteous actions are his own, they are always produced by the grace imparted to him, and he never dares to take any credit for them! He sings, "Not to us, O LORD, not to us, but to your name give glory" (Ps. 115:1). If he fails, he blames himself; if he succeeds, he glorifies God! Imitate the righteous man's example—lay every fault, every weakness, and every infirmity at your own door, and if you fall in any respect short of perfection—and I am sure you do—take all that to yourself and do not excuse yourself. But if there is any virtue, any praise, any true desire, any real prayer—*anything* that is good—ascribe it all to the Spirit of God! Remember, the righteous man would not be righteous unless God had made him righteous, and the fruit of God's righteousness would never come from him unless the divine sap within him had produced that acceptable fruit. To God alone is all honor and glory!

The main lesson of the passage is that this outburst of life from the Christian, this consequence of life within him, *this fruit of his soul becomes a blessing to others*. Like a tree, it yields shade and sustenance to all around. It is a tree of life, an expression I cannot fully work out tonight as I would wish, for there is a world of instruction compressed into the illustration. That which to the believer himself is fruit becomes to others a tree—it is a singular metaphor, but by no means a lame one. From the child of God there falls the fruit of holy living, even as an acorn drops from the oak; this holy living becomes influential and produces the best results in others, even as the acorn becomes itself an oak and lends its shade to the birds of the air. The Christian's holiness becomes a tree of life. I suppose it means a living tree, a tree calculated to give life and sustenance to others. A fruit becomes a tree! A tree of life! What a wonderful result! Christ *in the Christian* produces a character that becomes a tree of life. The outward character is the fruit of the inner life—this outer life itself grows from a fruit into a tree, and as a tree, it bears fruit in others to the praise and glory of God.

Dear brothers and sisters, I know some of God's saints who live very near to him, and they are evidently a tree of life for their very shadow is comforting, cooling, and refreshing to many weary souls. I have known the young and the tried; the downcast go to them, sit beneath their shade, and pour out their troubles. They have felt it a rich blessing to receive their sympathy, to be told of the faithfulness of the Lord, and to be guided in the way of his wisdom. There are a few good men in this world whom to know is to be rich; such men are libraries of gospel truths, but they are better than books for the truth of God in them is written on *living* pages! Their character is a true and living tree—it is not a mere post of the dead wood of doctrine bearing an inscription, and rotting at the same time, but it is a vital, organized, fruit-producing thing—a plant of the Lord's right hand planting!

Not only do some saints give comfort to others but they also yield them spiritual nourishment. Well-trained Christians become nursing fathers and nursing mothers, strengthening the weak and binding up the wounds of the brokenhearted. So, too, the strong, bold, generous deeds of large-hearted Christians are of great service to their fellow Christians and tend to raise them to a higher level. You feel refreshed by observing how they *act*—their patience in suffering, their courage in danger, their holy faith in God, their happy faces under trial. In a thousand ways the sanctified believer's example acts in a healing and comforting way to his brothers and sisters and assists in raising them above anxiety and unbelief. Even as the leaves of the tree of life are for the healing of the people, so the words and deeds of saints are medicine for a thousand maladies.

And then what fruit instructed believers bear! They are sweet to the taste of the godly. We can never trust in men as we trust in the Lord, but the Lord can cause the members to bless us in their measure, even as their head is ever ready to do. Jesus alone is the tree of life, but he makes some of his servants to be instrumental to us little trees of life, by whom he gives us fruit of the same sort that he bears himself, for he puts it there, and it is *himself* in his saints causing them to bring portly golden apples with which our souls are gladdened! May every one of us be made like our Lord, and may his fruit be found upon our branches!

We have put into the tomb, during the last year, many of the saints who have fallen asleep. Among them there were some of whom I will not at this moment particularly speak—whose lives, as I look back upon them, are still a tree of life to me. I pray God that I may be like them! Many of you knew them, and if you will only recall their holy, devoted lives, the influence they have left behind will still be a tree of life to you. They being dead yet speak; hear their eloquent exhortations! Even in their ashes, live their blessed fires—kindle your souls in their warmth. Their noble examples are the endowments of this church! Its children are ennobled and enriched as they remember their walk of faith and labor of love. Beloved, may every one of us be true benedictions to the churches in whose gardens we are planted. "Oh," says one, "I am afraid I am not much like a tree, for I feel so weak and insignificant." If you have faith as a grain of mustard seed, you have the commencement of the tree beneath whose branches the birds of the air will yet find lodging. The very birds that would have eaten the tiny seed come and find lodging in the tree that grows out of it! And people who despise and mock you, now that you are a young beginner, will one of these days, if God blesses you, be glad to borrow comfort from your example and experience!

But one other thought on this point. Remember that *the completeness and development of the holy life will be seen above.* There is a city of which it is written, "Through the middle of the street of the city; also, on either side of the river, the tree of life" (Rev. 22:2). The tree of life is a heavenly plant, and so the fruit of the Christian is a thing of heaven! Though not transplanted to the glory land, it is getting fit for its final abode. What is holiness, but heaven on earth? What is living unto God, but the essence of heaven? What is uprightness, integrity, Christlikeness? Have not these, even more, to do with heaven than harps and palms, and streets of purest gold? Holiness, purity, loveliness of character—these make a heaven within a man's own bosom! And even if there were no place called heaven, that heart would have a heavenly happiness that is set free from sin and made like the Lord Jesus! See, then, dear brothers and sisters, what an important thing it is for us to be indeed righteous before God, for then the outcome of that righteousness shall be fruit that will be a tree of life to others, and a tree of life in heaven above, world without end. O blessed Spirit, make it so. And you shall have all the praise!

Soul-Winning Should Be Our Pursuit

For "he who wins souls is wise" (Prov. 11:30 NKJV). The two things are put together—the life first, the effort next—what God has joined together let no man put asunder.

It is implied in our text that there are souls that *need* winning. Ah me, all souls of men are lost by nature. You might walk through the streets of London and say of the masses of men you meet upon those crowded pavements with sighs and tears— "Lost, lost, lost!" Wherever Christ is not trusted—the Spirit has not created a new heart, and the soul has not come to the great Father—there is a lost soul. But here is the mercy—these lost souls can be won! They are not hopelessly lost! God has not yet determined that they shall forever abide as they are. It is not yet said, "He who is filthy, let him be filthy still" (Rev. 22:11 NKJV), but they are in the land of hope where God's mercy may reach them—for they are spoken of as capable of being won!

They may yet be delivered, but the phrase hints that it will need all our efforts. "He who *wins* souls." What do we mean by that word *win?* We use it in *courtship*; we speak of the bridegroom who *wins* his bride, and sometimes there is a large expanse of love, many a pleading word, and much wooing before the valued heart is the suitor's own. I use this explanation because, in some respects, it is the very best, for souls will have to be won for Christ in this fashion, that they may be married to him. We must woo the sinner for Christ—that is how hearts are to be won for him. Jesus is the bridegroom, and we must speak for him and tell of his beauty, as Abraham's servant, when he went to seek a wife for Isaac, acted as a wooer in his stead. Have you ever read the story? Then turn to it when you get home, and see how he talked about his master, what possessions he had, and how Isaac was to be head of it all, and so on. He then finished his address by urging Rebecca to go with him. The question was put to her, "Will you go with this man?" So, the minister's business is to commend his Master and his Master's riches, and then to say to souls, "Will you be wedded to Christ?" He who can succeed in this very delicate business is a wise man.

We also use the term in a *military* fashion. We speak of winning a city, a castle, or a battle. We do not win victories by going to sleep. Believe me, castles are not captured by men who are only half awake; to win a battle requires the best skills, the greatest endurance, and the utmost courage. To storm fortresses regarded as almost impregnable, men need to burn the midnight oil and study well the areas of attack. And when the time comes for the assault, not a soldier must be a laggard, but all force of artillery and manhood must be brought to bear on the point assailed. To carry a man's heart by main force of grace, to capture it, to break down the bars of brass and dash the gates of iron in pieces requires the exercise of a skill only Christ can give. To bring up the big battering rams and shake every stone in the sinner's conscience, to make his heart rock and reel within him for fear of the wrath to come, in a word, to assail a soul with all the artillery of the gospel needs a wise man—one awakened to his work! To hold up the white flag of God's mercy, and if that is despised, to use the battering ram of threats until a breach is made. Then with the Sword of the Spirit in his hand, to capture the city, to tear down the black flag of sin and run up the banner of the cross, needs all the force the most choice preacher can command, and a great deal more! Those whose souls are as cold as the Arctic regions and whose energy is reduced to the vanishing point are not likely to take the city of Mansoul for Prince Emmanuel. If you think you are going to win souls, you must throw your soul into your work, just as a warrior must throw his soul into a battle—or victory will not be yours.

We use the words "to win" in reference to *making a fortune,* and we all know that the man who becomes a millionaire must rise early, stay up late, and eat the bread of carefulness. We know it takes a deal of toiling and saving, and I know not what besides, to amass immense wealth. We have to go in for winning souls with the same ardor and concentration of our faculties as old Astor of New York went in to build up that fortune of so many millions, which he has now left behind him. It is indeed a race, and you know that in a race nobody wins unless he strains every muscle and sinew. They who run in a race all run, but only one receives the prize—and that one is generally he who had more strength than the rest. Certainly, whether he had more strength or not, he put out all he had, and we will not win souls unless we imitate him in this.

Solomon declares in the text that "he who wins souls is wise," and such a declaration is all the more valuable as coming from so wise a man. Let me show you why a true soul-winner is wise. First, *he must be taught of God before he will attempt it.* The man who does not know that he was once blind but now sees had better think of his own blindness before he attempts to lead his friends in the right way. If not saved yourself, you cannot be the means of saving others! He that wins souls must be wise unto salvation first for himself. That being taken for granted, *he is a wise man to select such a pursuit.* Young man, are you choosing an objective worthy to be the great aim of your life? I do hope you will judge wisely and select a noble ambition. If God has given you great gifts, I hope they will not be used on any low, wretched, or selfish design.

Suppose I am now addressing one who has great talents and has an opportunity of being what he likes—of going into Parliament and helping to pass wise measures or of going into business and making himself a man of importance. I hope he will weigh the claims of Jesus and immortal souls as well as other claims. Should I addict myself to study? Should I surrender myself to business? Should I travel? Should I spend my time in pleasure? Should I become the principal fox hunter of the county? Should I lay out my time in promoting political and social reforms? Think them all over, but if you are a Christian, my dear friend, nothing will equal in enjoyment, in usefulness, in honor, and in lasting recompense, the giving yourself up to the winning of souls! Oh, it is grand hunting, I can tell you, and beats all the fox hunting in the world in excitement and exhilaration! Have I not sometimes gone with a cry over hedge and ditch after some poor sinner and kept up with him in every twist and turn he took until I have overtaken him, by God's grace, and been in at the death, and rejoiced exceedingly when I have seen him captured by my Master? Our Lord Jesus calls his ministers fishermen, and no other fishermen have such labor, such sorrow, and such delight as we have! What a happy thing it is that you may win souls for Jesus and may do this though you abide in your secular callings. Some of you would never win souls in pulpits—it would be a great pity if you tried—but you can win souls in the workshop, in the laundry, in the nursery, and in the drawing room! Our hunting grounds are everywhere—by the wayside, by the fireside, in the corner, and in the crowd. Among the common people, Jesus is our theme, and among the great ones, we have no other. You will be wise, my brothers, if for you the one absorbing desire is that you may turn the ungodly from the error of their ways. For you there will be a crown glittering with many stars that you will cast at Jesus's feet in the day of his appearing!

Further, it is not only wise to make this your aim, *but you will have to be very wise if you succeed in it* because the souls to be won are so different in their constitutions, feelings, and conditions, and you will have to adapt yourselves to them all! The trappers of North America have to find out the habits of the animals they wish to catch—and so you will have to learn how to deal with each class of sinners. Some are very depressed; you will have to comfort them. Perhaps you will comfort them too much, and make them unbelieving, and, therefore, possibly instead of comforting them, you will need sometimes to administer a sharp word to cure the sulkiness into which they have fallen.

Another person may be frivolous. If you put on a serious face, you will frighten your bird away—you will have to be cheerful and drop a word of admonition, as if by accident. Some people again will not let *you* speak to them but will talk to you! You must know the art of putting a word in edgeways! You will have to be very wise and become all things to all men, but your success will prove your wisdom. Theories of dealing with souls may look very wise, but they often prove to be useless when actually tried. He who by God's grace accomplishes the work is a wise man, though perhaps he knows no theory whatsoever. This work will need all your wit, and far more, and you will have to cry to the great Winner of Souls above to give you of his Holy Spirit.

But, mark you—he that wins souls is wise because *he is engaged in a business that makes men wiser as they proceed with it.* You will bungle at first and very likely drive sinners off from Christ by your attempts to draw them to him. I have tried to move some souls with all my might with a certain passage of Scripture, but they have taken it in an opposite light to what it was intended and have steered off in the wrong direction. It is very difficult to know how to act with bewildered inquirers. If you want some people to go forward, you must pull them backward. If you want them to go to the right, you must insist upon their going to the left, but by God's grace they go to the right directly. You must be ready for these follies of poor human nature. I know a poor aged Christian woman who had been a child of God fifty years, but she was in a state of melancholy and distress, from which nobody could awaken her. I called several times, and endeavored to cheer her up, but generally, when I

left, she was worse than before. So, one time I called to see her.
I did not say anything to her about Christ or religion. She soon
introduced those topics herself, and then I remarked that I was
not going to talk to her about such holy things for she did not
know anything about them. I told her she was not a believer in
Christ and had been no doubt a hypocrite for many years. She
could not stand that, and asserted, in self-defense, that the Lord
above knew her better than I did, and *he* was her witness that she
did love the Lord Jesus Christ. She scarcely forgave herself afterward for that admission, but she could never talk to me quite so
despairingly anymore! True lovers of men's souls learn the art of
dealing with them, and the Holy Spirit makes them expert soul
surgeons for Jesus. It is not because a man has more abilities, nor
altogether because he has more grace, but the *Lord* makes him
to love the souls of men intensely, and this imparts a secret skill,
since for the most part, the way to get sinners to Christ is to *love
them* to Christ.

Beloved brothers, I will say once more, *he who really wins
souls for Jesus, however he wins them, is a wise man.* Some of you
are slow to admit this. You say, "Well, so-and-so, I dare say, has
been very useful, but he is very rough." What does his roughness
matter if he wins souls? "Ah," says another, "but I am not built
up under him." Why do you go to hear him? To be built up? If
the Lord has sent him to pull down, let him pull down! And you
go elsewhere for edification, but do not grumble at a man who
does one work because he cannot do another! We are also too
apt to pit one minister against another and say, "You should hear
my minister." Perhaps we should, but it would be better for *you*
to hear the man who edifies you, and let others go where they
also are instructed. "He who wins souls is wise." I do not ask you
how he did it. He sang the gospel, and you did not like it, but
if he won souls, he was wise! Soul-winners all have their own
ways, and if they do but win souls, they are wise. I will tell you
what is *not* wise and will not be thought so at the last—namely,
to go about the churches doing nothing yourself and railing at all
the Lord's useful servants! Here is a dear brother on his dying
bed; he has the sweet thought that the Lord enabled him to

bring many souls to Jesus and the expectation when he comes to the gates that many spirits will come to meet him. They will throng the ascent to the New Jerusalem and welcome the man who brought them to Jesus! They are immortal monuments to his labors; he is wise. Here is another who has spent all his time in interpreting the prophecies so that everything he reads in the newspapers, he could see in Daniel or Revelation. He is wise, so some say, but I had rather spend my time in winning souls! I would sooner bring one sinner to Jesus Christ than unpick all the mysteries of the divine Word, for salvation is the thing we are to live for! I would to God that I understood all mysteries, yet chief of all, would I proclaim the mystery of soul-saving by faith in the blood of the Lamb! It is comparatively a small matter for a minister to have been a staunch upholder of orthodoxy all his days and to have spent himself in keeping up the hedges of his church. Soul-winning is the main concern!

It is a very good thing to contend earnestly for the faith once delivered to the saints, but I do not think I should like to say in my last account, "Lord, I have lived to fight the Romanists and the State church and to put down the various erroneous sects, but I never led a sinner to the cross." No, we will fight the good fight of faith, but the winning of souls is the greater matter—he who attends to it is wise! Another brother has preached the truth of God, but he did so polish up his sermons that the gospel was hidden. Never a sermon was fit to preach, he thought, until he had written it out a dozen times to see whether every sentence would be according to the canons of Cicero and Quintilian— and then he went and delivered the gospel as a grand oration. Is that wise? Well, it takes a wise man to be a thorough orator, but it is better not to be an orator if fine speech prevents your being understood! Let eloquence be flung to the dogs rather than souls lost! What we need is to win souls, and they are not to be won by flowery speeches! We must have the winning of souls at heart and be red hot with zeal for their salvation—then, however much we blunder, according to the critics; we will be numbered among those whom the *Lord* calls wise!

Now, Christian men and women, I want you to take this matter up practically and to determine that you will try this very night to win a soul! Try the one next to you in the pew if you cannot think of anybody else. Try on the way home; try with your own children. Have I not told you of what happened one Sunday six months ago? In my sermon I said, "Now, you mothers, have you ever prayed with each of your children, one by one, and urged them to lay hold on Christ? Perhaps dear Jane is now in bed, and you have never yet pleaded with her about eternal things. Go home tonight, wake her up, and say, "Jane, I am sorry I have never personally told you about the Savior, and prayed with you, but I mean to do it now. Wake her up, and put your arms round her neck, and pour out your heart to God with her!" Well, there was a good sister here who had a daughter named Jane. What do you think? She came on Monday to bring her daughter Jane to see me in the vestry, for when she woke her up and began, "I have not spoken to you about Jesus," or something to that effect, "Oh, dear mother," said Jane, "I have loved the Savior these six months and wondered why you had not spoken to me about him." And then there was such kissing and rejoicing! Perhaps you may find that to be the case with a dear child at home, but if you do not, so much more the reason why you should begin at once to speak! Did you never win a soul for Jesus? You will have a crown in heaven, but no jewels in it! You will go to heaven childless! And you know how it was in the old times, how the women dreaded lest they should be childless! Let it be so with Christian people! Let them dread being spiritually childless! We *must* hear the cries of those whom God has given to be born unto himself by our means! We *must* hear them, or else cry out in anguish, "Give me converts, or I die!" Young men, old men, and sisters of all ages, if you love the Lord, get a passion for souls! Do you not see them? They are going down to hell by the thousands! As often as the hand upon the dial completes its circuit, hell devours multitudes! Some of them are ignorant of Christ, and others willfully reject him! The world lies in darkness—this great city still pines for the light of God! Your own friends and family may be dead before this week is over! Oh, if you have any humanity, let alone Christianity, if you have found the remedy, *tell* the diseased about it! If you have found life, proclaim it to the dead! If you have found liberty, publish it to the captives! If you have found Christ, tell of him to others! My brothers in the college, let this be your choice work while studying, and let it be the one objective of your lives when you go forth from us. Do not be content when you get a congregation, but labor to *win souls*, and as you do this, God will bless you. As for us, we hope during the rest of our lives to follow him who is *the* soul-winner, and to put ourselves in his hands who makes *us* soul-winners, so that our life may not be a long folly but may be proven by results to have been directed by his wisdom!

O you souls not won to Jesus, remember that faith in Christ saves you! Trust in him! May you be led to trust in him for his name's sake. Amen.

Sermon #8

The Marvelous Magnet

**No. 1717, Metropolitan Tabernacle, London, England,
when the regular hearers left their seats
to be occupied by strangers.**

*And I, when I am lifted up from the earth, will draw
all people to myself." He said this to show by
what kind of death he was going to die.*
– John 12:32–33

Jesus is the spokesman here. He tells of his own death by crucifixion and of the result that will follow. It appears, then, that our
Lord's power to draw all men to himself lies mainly in his death.
By being lifted up from the earth on the cross, he was made to
die, and he also was made to draw all men to himself. There is
an attractive power about our Lord's person and about his life
teaching. But, still, the main attractive force lies in his death on
the cross. Most certainly, this is rare and strange, for when a
great religious leader dies, a large measure of his personal power
is gone. The charm of the man's manner, the impressiveness of
his personal conviction, the lofty tone of his daily enthusiasm—
these are immense helps to a cause while they are with us. To
lose them is a fearful drawback such as makes it perilous for a
religious leader to die. Men may remember a leader's life for a
time after his death. They will do so most emphatically if he has

143

been eminently good. We say of the righteous, "Even in their ashes live their usual fires." From many a tomb there rises a silent voice more eloquent than the choicest speech, "He being dead yet speaks." But there is a measure and boundary to the influence of a mere memory. How often it is the case that, after a little while, the leader having gone, the feebler folk gradually drop away, the hypocritical openly desert, the lukewarm wander, and so the cause dies out. The man's successors desert his principles, or maintain them with but little life and energy, and therefore, what was once a hopeful effort expires like a dying taper. For a man's work to prosper, it is not desirable that he should die. Is it not strange that what is so often fatal to the influence of other men is a gain to our Lord Jesus Christ? For it is by his death that he possesses his most powerful influence over the sons of men. Because Jesus died, he is to this day the mightiest ruler of human minds, the great center to which all hearts are being drawn.

Remember, too, that our Lord Jesus Christ died by a most shameful death. We have come to use the cross as an ornament, and by some it is regarded as an object of reverence. But the cross, to speak very plainly, was to the ancients what the gallows are to us—an odious instrument of death for felons—exactly that and no more. The death on a cross was one never allotted to a Roman citizen except for certain heinous crimes. It was regarded as the death penalty of a slave. It was not only painful, it was disgraceful and shameful. And to say that a man was crucified was, in our Lord's time, tantamount to saying in our speech today that he was hanged. It means just that, and you must accept the death of the cross with all the shame that can be connected with the gallows and the tree of death, or else you will not understand what it meant to Jesus and his disciples.

Now, surely, if a man is hanged, there is an end to his influence among men. When I was looking through all the Bible commentaries in the English language, I found one with a title page attributing it to Dr. Coke. But on further examination I perceived that it was the commentary of Dr. Dodd, who was executed for forgery. After he had been hanged, of course the publishers could not sell a commentary under his name, and so they engaged another learned doctor to take it under his wing. The man was hanged, and therefore, people would not read his book, and you are not at all surprised that it should be so. But here is an amazing thing. The Lord Jesus has lost no influence by having been hanged on the cross. No, rather it is because of his shameful death that he is able to draw all men to himself. His glory rises from his humiliation, his adorable conquest from his shameful death. When he "[became] obedient to the point of death, even death on a cross," shame cast no shame upon his cause but gilded it with glory. Christ's death of weakness threw no weakness into Christianity. Say rather that it is the right arm of its power. By the sign of suffering unto death, the church has conquered and will conquer still. By a love which is strong as death, it has always been victorious, and must forever remain so. When it has not been ashamed to put the cross in the forefront, it has never had to be ashamed, for God has been with it, and Jesus has drawn all men to himself. The crucified Christ has irresistible attractions. When he stoops into the utmost suffering and scorn, even the brutal must relent. A living Savior men *may* love, but a crucified Savior they *must* love. If they perceive that he loved them and gave himself for them, their hearts are stolen away. The city of Mansoul is captured before the siege begins, when the Prince Emmanuel uncovers the beauties of his dying love before the eyes of the rebellious ones.

Let us never be ashamed, dear friends, to preach Christ crucified—the Son of God lifted up to die among the condemned. Let those of us who teach in the Sunday school or preach at the street corner or in any other manner try to set forth the gospel, always keep a dying Christ to the front. Christ without the cross is no Christ at all. Never forget that he is the eternal God, but bind with that truth the fact that he was nailed to a Roman cross. It is on the tree he triumphed over Satan, and it is by the cross that he must triumph over the world. "'And I, when I am lifted up from the earth, will draw all people to myself.' He said this to show by what kind of death he was going to die."

The Attractiveness of the Crucified Savior

You will observe that it is briefly summed up in these words—
himself to *himself*. *"I* will draw all people to *myself."* It is not written that Christ will draw all men to the visible church, for the
universal profession of our holy faith is slow enough in coming.
Certainly, the Lord Jesus Christ will not lend himself out to draw
men to your sect or to mine. He will draw always toward truth
and righteousness, but not to dead forms or meaningless distinc-
tions nor to the memories of former wrongs or party victories. If
the Lord should draw men to the cathedral or the tabernacle, the
abbey or the chapel, it would be of little service to them, unless
in each case they found him. The main thing that is needed is
that they be drawn to him, and none can draw them to him but
him. Himself drawing them to himself—this is the soul of the
text.

I dare say that you have heard the oft-recounted story of the
missionaries among the Greenlanders. Our Moravian brethren,
full of fire and zeal and self-denial, went right away among the
ignorant folk of Greenland, as those people then were, longing
to convert them. Using large prudence, they thought, "These
people are so unenlightened that it cannot be of any use to
preach Jesus Christ to them at first. They do not even know that
there is a God, so let us begin by teaching them the nature of the
Deity, showing them right and wrong, proving to them the need
of atonement for sin, and setting before them the rewards of the
righteous and the penalties of the wicked." This was judged to
be most fit preparatory work. Watch for the result! They went on
for years but had no converts. What was there in all that fine preparatory teaching that could convert anybody? Jesus was being
locked out of the Greenlanders' hearts by those who wanted him
to enter.

But one day, one of the missionaries happened to read to a
poor Greenlander the story of Jesus bleeding on the cross and
how God had sent his Son to die, "that whoever believes in him
should not perish, but have everlasting life." And the Greenlander
said, "Would you read me that again? What wonderful words!

Did the Son of God die for us poor Greenlanders that we may live?" The missionary answered that it was even so, and clapping his hands, the simple native cried, "Why did you not tell us that before?" Ah, just so! Why not tell them this at once, and leave it to clear its own path? That is the point to begin with. Let us start with the Lamb of God who takes away the sin of the world. "God so loved the world that he gave his only begotten Son, that whoever believes in him should not perish, but have everlasting life." To my mind, that is the point to begin with and the point to go on with; yes, that is the truth to conclude with, if there can ever be any conclusion to the grand old story of the incarnate God who loved his enemies and gave himself to die in their place, that they might live through him. The gospel is Jesus drawing sinners to himself that they might live through him. Dear hearers, do you know what this means? I know that many of you do, and you are happy, for in this knowledge there is life. Would to God that all knew this power of love in Christ, knew it so as to be drawn by almighty love to return that love with all their heart and soul and strength. The best thing that can happen to any of us is to feel Christ drawing him to Christ and to find himself sweetly yielding to the gentle drawing of the Savior's love.

The text says that Jesus Christ will draw all men unto himself. Now, all men who hear of Jesus Christ at all are drawn, but they do not all yield. Some of them pull back, and the worst thing that can happen to a man is when he pulls back until Jesus lets him go. What a fall is that, when the drawing power is taken away and the man falls backward into destruction, which he himself has chosen, having refused eternal life and resisted the Savior's power! Unhappy is the wretch who strives against his own salvation. Every man who hears the gospel feels some measure of its drawing power. I appeal to any one of you who has been accustomed to hearing it. Does not Jesus sometimes tug hard at your conscience, and though you have pulled back, yet has he not drawn and drawn again? I remember how he drew *me* as a child, though I drew back from him, yet he never let me go until he drew me over the borderline. Some of you must well remember how you were drawn by a mother's gentle words, by a teacher's earnest pleadings, by a father's admonitions, by a sister's tears, by a pastor's entreaties. Permit your memories to aid me. Bring up before your mind's eye the many dear ones who have broken their hearts to win you for Jesus. Yes, you have been drawn.

I suppose all of you have felt a measure of that drawing. Why, it is not merely those who hear the gospel but whole nations have been drawn, in other respects, by the all-pervading influence of Jesus and his love. At this instant, the influence of Christianity is being felt in every corner of the earth to an extent that it is not easy to exaggerate. If I had an orator's power, I would picture my Savior casting golden chains of love over all nations, wherever the missionary goes preaching his name. The Lord is taming the nations as a man by degrees; he subdues wild beasts. Jesus is gradually drawing the heathen to himself. He has had a long tug at India. That dead weight still lies in the furrow. But it must come. It must yield. All those who watch it know that if there is any cause that makes progress in India, it is the cause of Christ. The East appears never to move, but if there is any move, it is Christward. Jesus is drawing China slowly. Japan is being drawn as in a net. Where the testimony of Christ has been borne, the idols begin to shake and their priests confess that a change is coming. Every century sees a marked advance in the world's condition, and we will progress at a quicker rate yet when the church wakes up to a sense of its responsibility and the Holy Spirit is poured out on the church to turn us all into missionaries, causing us all in some way or other to preach the gospel of Christ. Jesus is drawing, drawing, drawing. When God meant to scatter the individuals of our race, they would not be scattered; they built a tower to be the center of union. And only by their tongues being so changed that they could not understand one another could their resolve to remain in one company be defeated. But now, behold, the whole earth has the race of men to cover it. The sons of Adam dwell in every region, and it is the Father's will to gather together in one the redeemed of the Lord. Therefore, he has set in their midst the great Shiloh, of whom it was prophesied of old, "To him shall the gathering of the people be." The roaming races do not answer to the Father's call. They do not want to come to the elder Brother's rule, but they will have to come, for he must reign. Gentile and Jew, African and European—they will all meet at the cross, the common center of our entire humanity, for Christ is lifted up, and he is drawing all men to himself.

But all men are not saved. No, for when drawn, they do not come. Yet Christ crucified is drawing some men of all kinds and sorts to eternal life. When Jesus died on the cross, it was not for my lord and lady only, nor was it only for the working man; it was for all sorts of people—

> While grace is offered to the prince,
> The poor may take their share.
> No mortal has a just pretense
> To perish in despair.

He who is best taught and instructed has often been drawn to Jesus by the Lord's overpowering charms. Some of the most learned of men have been delighted to come to Christ. But the most illiterate and rude have equally been drawn by Jesus, and it has been their joy to come. I love to hear of the gospel being preached to the poorest of the poor, and so preached that it reaches those who never were reached by it before. Godspeed every effort by which Jesus is set before the fallen and degraded. So long as it is the gospel and not mere rant, we wish Godspeed to the most irregular of witnesses. Our fears begin only when Jesus is no longer in the front. We greatly need to have the gospel preached in the west of London, and so preached that our great ones may receive it and find life through Jesus Christ. May such a movement soon take place. How I should like to hear of a converted duke telling out the gospel or a reclaimed knight of the garter proclaiming mercy for the chief of sinners! Why not? And blessed be God the Savior, lifted up, draws all sorts of men to himself—some of every kind, not the Jew alone, as at the first, but the Gentile too!

None are excluded but those,
Who do themselves exclude.
Welcome the learned and polite,
The ignorant and rude.

There is no exclusion of any class or creature from the mercy of God in Christ Jesus. "I, when I am lifted up from the earth, will draw all people to myself," and the history of the church proves how true this is. The assembly roll of the converted includes princes and paupers, peers and ale men.

But what is this force that attracts men to the crucified Savior? They do come. There is no doubt about it. Look, sirs, there is nothing in the world that men will hear so gladly as the gospel. How many years have I stood in this place to preach to a congregation precisely similar to the present! The crowds have been here as regularly as the hours, Sunday after Sunday, morning and evening, year after year. Suppose that I had been appointed to preach upon a scientific subject? Could I have gained or held such audiences? I should have been spun out a long while ago if I had been bound to draw upon myself for my matter. If I had preached any other than the doctrine of Christ crucified, I should years ago have scattered my audience to the winds of heaven. But the old theme is always new, always fresh, always attractive. Preach Jesus Christ. That is the recipe for catching men's ears and laying hold of men's hearts. The name of Jesus is to man's heart the mightiest of charms. Man's ears wait for it as the morning hour waits for the sun or as the parched earth waits for the shower. Ring out the name of Jesus; it is the sweetest carol ever sung. Ring it out without fear or stint, for it is always welcome as the flowers in May. Men will never tire of it until the flowers are satiated with sunlight and the grass grows weary of the dew. The music of that blessed silver bell rings out over hill and dale as sweetly as when, on the first Christmas night, the angels sang, "Glory to God in the highest, and on earth peace, good will toward men." There is about Calvary and its infinite stoop of divine love a power that never dies out, and never will while the world stands. What is it? From where does this universal attractiveness come?

Well, first, it is the force of *love*, for Jesus Christ is incarnate love. In him, you see one who divested himself of all his glory, that he might save the guilty, who came down upon earth, not seeking wealth and fame but simply seeking to do good by saving men; who, having laid aside his honor and his glory, at last laid aside his life, and all for love, for love that met a sad return, for love that has, however, saved its objectives with a great salvation. One of the school men says that whenever we know that another person loves us, we cannot help giving back a measure of love in return, and I believe that the statement is true. Certainly, such love as the love of Christ, when it is told out simply, and men can understand it, is certain to excite an interest, to win a degree of attention, and so to lead up to better things. Full often this love proves its power over observers by transforming them from enemies into friends, and though they at first despised the Redeemer, his love compels them, at length, to believe and to adore. If I were asked the secret of the attracting power of the crucified Savior, I would answer that it is invincible love. The only crime that ever could be laid to Jesus's charge was that of which the poet sings—"found guilty of excessive love"—loving beyond all reason and beyond all bounds—loving as none ever loved before, so that if all the rivers of human love ran together, they could not fill such an ocean of love as was in the heart of Jesus the Savior. This it is—this unique, unrivaled love—that draws men to Jesus. The pierced heart of Christ is a magnet to draw all other hearts.

No doubt there is also this about the crucified Savior—that he draws men by *the wonderful rest his death provides for men.* The most earnest Christian man must sometimes have his doubts as to whether all is right with him. The sincerer a man is, the more does he tremble lest he should deceive himself. You, good brother, have your personal anxieties; certainly, I have mine. But when I turn my eyes to Jesus upon the cross and view the crown of thorns, the sacred head, the eyes that were red with weeping, the hands nailed fast to the wood, and the feet dripping with blood, when I remember that this shameful death was endured for love of me, I am so quiet and so happy in my spirit that I cannot tell how peacefully my life-floods flow. God *must* forgive my grievous fault, for my Redeemer has so grievously answered for it. When I see Jesus die, I perceive that from now on divine justice is on the sinner's side. How can the Lord God punish the same offense twice—first the Substitute and then the men for whom that Substitute has bled? Christ has bled as substitute for every man that believes in him—every believer is therefore safe. Oh, brethren, when you are troubled, rest with us by looking to Calvary. And if the first glance does not quiet you, look, and look, and look again, for every grief will die where Jesus died. Not to Bethlehem, where the stars of Christmas burn, do we look for our greatest comfort but to that place where the sun was darkened at midday and the face of eternal love was veiled. Because the Lord of life and glory was dying *in extremis,* suffering the deadliest pain for our sakes, therefore his wounds distilled the richest balm that ever healed a sinner's wound. Men know this. Reading their Bibles, they soon find it out. There is no comfort for them against the anger of God and against their guilty consciences until they see Christ in their place, suffering for them. The conscience sees, with unspeakable delight, the victim provided. It gladly lays its hand on Jesus's head, and sees its sin transferred to him and punished in him, and thus it finds rest, like the rest of God. In the expiatory death of Jesus, the law is vindicated, and God is "just and the justifier of the one who has faith in Jesus" (Rom. 3:26).

Dear friends, believe me, Jesus bestows the peerless pearl of perfect rest on every heart that comes to him. He fills the soul so that it has no more longings. You know the horseshoe magnet, and you have seen how rapidly it picks up pieces of iron. Have you ever put a piece of iron right across the two ends of the magnet? You will then have noticed that it ceases to attract anything else. The magnetic circuit is completed, and the magnet rests perfectly quiet, refusing to go beyond its own circle of pure content. When my soul is filled with Jesus, he completes the circuit of my soul's passions and longings. He is all my salvation and all my desire. Have you found it so? Has not your soul come to an absolutely perfect rest when it has gotten to Christ? When he himself has drawn you to himself, have you not entered into rest? Because men perceive that such a rest is to be had, therefore, they come to Christ. He himself uses this as an argument why they should come. Remember his cheering words, "Come to me, all who labor and are heavy laden, and I will give you rest" (Matt. 11:28). This is part of the attractive force that dwells in the crucified Savior.

Then I am sure there is a great attraction about Christ when we see *the change which he works in men.* Have you known a drunk become a Christian or a thief become upright? Have you seen a harlot made chaste? Have you marked any of the modern miracles that are always going on around us in the form of conversions? If you have taken pleasure in these signs and wonders, I know that you have said, "Lord, I too will come to you to be converted." The sight of his power to elevate and sanctify has attracted you to Jesus, and you have fallen at his feet. There is no true, deep, tender, living conversion except through the cross, and therefore those who are taught of God do love to come to Christ so that sin may be conquered in them, that the heart of stone may be taken away, that the heart of flesh may be given, and that they may walk the happy way of holiness, according to the example of their adorable Master.

I could continue thus to show what this attractive force is, but lest I should weary you, I will only say that it lies much in *his sufferings themselves.* Is it not a strange thing that suffering attracts? Yes, more, lowly suffering conquers. She sits as a queen upon her throne, and reigns by the royalty of her resignation. The ship of the church has plowed its way through seas of blood. With the blood-red cross at the masthead, she has pushed on even in the night, throwing the crimson spray about her. She has never paused because of persecution, affliction, or death. These are the rough winds that fill her sails. No progress is surer than that which comes of holy suffering. The enemies of the church have taken its disciples and burned them, but their deaths yielded a sweet savor of life. It is questionable if a man's influence can be better promoted than by sending him aloft in a chariot of fire. What made us a Protestant nation for so many years? I do not say that we are Protestant now, but what made us enthusiastically anti-papist for so many years? The stakes of Smithfield did it. Men and women stood and saw the martyrs burned, and as they saw them die, they said, "These men are right, and the cause for which they burn is true." And into the very heart of England martyrdom cast up a way for the Lord Jesus, and he entered then and there into Old England's secret soul. What the martyrs did in their measure, by their bitter death-pangs, is being done on a divine scale by the sufferings of the chief of all martyrs and head of all witnesses. By the agonies of Jesus, men's affections are moved and their hearts enthralled.

Are any of you unconverted, and do you wish to be converted? I cannot suggest a better exercise than to read over the story of the death of Christ, as it is told by the four Evangelists. When you have read it once, read it again. And as you read it, say, "Lord, I must have a sadly hard heart, or else this would move me to tears. I pray, change my heart." Then read the story again, for sure, at last, it will touch you. God the Holy Spirit blessing you, it will move you, and you will be among the "all men" that will be drawn to Jesus by his own personal force so much, then, about what this force is.

How Is This Force Exercised?

This force is exercised through the Holy Spirit. It is the Spirit of God who puts power into the truth about Christ. And then men feel that truth and come to Christ and live. But our blessed Lord and Master *uses instruments.* The force of Christ's love is sometimes shown to men by those who already love him. One Christian makes many. One believer leads others to faith. To come back to my metaphor of a magnet, you have sometimes seen a battery attached to a coil, and then, if you take a nail and put it on the coil, the nail has become a strong magnet. You notice that the nail turns into a magnet, for you take another nail and put it on the end of it, and it holds the second nail fast. Now number two is turned into a magnet. Try it. Put a third nail upon it. See, it is held fast! Number three has become a magnet. Try the next nail, it holds on to it like grim death, and now number four has become a magnet. Bring another nail within the influence. Number five has become a magnet. And so, it continues. On and on and on, the magnetism goes, from one nail to another. But now, just go to your battery, and detach one of your wires, and the nails drop off directly, for the coil has ceased to be a magnet, and the nails have ceased to be magnets too. All the magnetism comes from the first place from which it started, and when it ceases at the fountainhead, there is an end of it altogether. Indeed, Jesus Christ is the great attractive magnet, and all must begin and end with him. When Jesus lays hold upon us, we get hold of a brother, and before long, he turns into a magnet also. Thus, from one to another the mystic influence proceeds, but the whole of the force abides in Jesus. More and more the kingdom grows, "ever mighty to prevail," but all the growing and the prevailing come out of him. So it is that Jesus works—first by himself, and then by all who are in him. May the Lord make us all magnets for himself. Jesus says, "I, when I am lifted up from the earth, will draw all people to myself," but he leaves room in his figure for the co-working of all grateful hearts.

Jesus draws men *gradually*. Some are brought to Christ in a moment, but many are drawn by slow degrees. The sun in some parts of the world rises above the horizon in a single instant. But in our own country, at this season of the year, it is beautiful to watch the dawn, from the first gray light to the actual break of day. Is it dark, or is it light? Well, it is not quite dark; it is visible darkness. By-and-by there is light. No sun is up as yet, but yet, the light increases until the east begins to glow and the west reflects the radiance. Then, by-and-by, up rises the great king of day. So does the Lord bring many to himself by gentle degrees. They cannot tell when they were converted, but they are converted, for they have come to Christ. Rest assured that he will not send you back. Do not say, "I am not converted, for I do not know the moment of the great change." I knew an old lady once who did not know her birthday, but I never told her that she was not born because of that, for there she was. And if you do not know when you were made a Christian, yet, if you are a Christian, it little matters how. If you are really born of God, the date of your new birth is interesting to curiosity but not important to piety. Salvation is often accomplished by a lengthened process. I have heard that when they wanted to bridge a great chasm, they shot across the river an arrow or a bullet that drew with it a tiny thread. That was all the communication from bank to bank, and the rolling torrent was far below. Despise not the day of small things! The insignificant beginning was prophetic of grand results. Through that little thread they drew across a piece of twine, and when they had safely grasped it on the other side, they bound a small rope to the end of the twine, and then they drew the rope across. Then to that rope they tied a cable, and they drew the cable across, and now over that chasm there strides an iron bridge, along which the steam horse rattles with his mighty load. So does Jesus unite us to himself. He may employ at first an insignificant thread of thought, then a sense of pleasant interest, some deeper feeling, a crushing emotion, a faint faith, a stronger faith, then stronger yet, until, at last, we come to be firmly bound to Christ. Oh, be thankful if you have only a thread of communication between you and Jesus, for it will lead to more. Something more hopeful will be drawn across the gulf before long; at least I hunger to see it. Christ's attractions are often very gradually revealed, and their victorious energy is not felt all at once.

Moreover, the cords of our Lord's drawings are very *secret*. You see the swallows twittering round our roofs, hawking in the air, shooting up into the clouds, or flashing by our ear. It is summer, and they are paying us their annual visit. They will be with us for a time, but all of a sudden, we will see them getting together about the gable of an old house, holding agitated congregations and evidently discussing matters of importance. The Lord of birds is gently drawing every swallow in England down toward the African coast, and they will all go, without exception, as the secret summons reaches the flying host. They know but little of the way, but their flight is not therefore delayed or its course left to uncertainty. Over thousands of miles of sea and land they pursue their course until they come to their resting place. And then, next spring, the same power that drew them southward will draw them all northward again. And here they will come, and we will hear their joyous twitter and say to ourselves, "Summer is coming, for here are the swallows again." By a secret power of that order does Jesus draw home the strangers and the foreigners whom his grace has chosen. They say to one another, "Come, and let us go up to the house of the Lord. Let us seek the face of the Savior." The mystic attractions of the power of Christ are secretly drawing many who knew him not, and now they ask their way to Zion with their faces Christward. Look how the sun draws along the planets. He hastens on in his mighty career in space—I know not where, but drawing with him all the worlds that compose the solar system. All these silently attend his majestic marches. Such is Christ, the great central sun, all his people follow, for he draws. Stand by the seashore and notice what the moon can do. You do not even see it, for it is high noon, but here comes a wave, and then another, and then another, and the tide rises a little higher today than it did yesterday. What is it that causes this pulse of life, these heartthrobs of the deep? The moon's attractive power is drawing up the waters from the sea. Even so our glorious Christ, in ways unknown to us, draws the hearts of men by his mighty Spirit wherever he pleases—"I, when I am lifted up from the earth, will draw all people to myself."

Fail not to observe *how gently* he does it! The classic heathen adored a goddess whom they represented as riding in a chariot drawn by doves. Surely the most tender mode of impulse—power without force, motion born of emotion! Certain of us were wafted to Jesus by some such zephyr. We could not but yield, the softness and tenderness of every touch of Jesus affected us infinitely more than force could possibly have done. Hearts are tender things and are not to be forced open with crowbars. The doors of the heart open gently to him who holds the key, and who is that but he who made the heart and bought it with his precious blood? The gentleness is equal to the power when Jesus draws men to himself!

But, oh, how *effectually!* I thought, as I mused upon my text, that I saw a great whirlpool like the maelstrom in the north of

Norway. I thought I saw an enormous whirlpool so huge that all the souls of men, like ships of many different forms, were being drawn toward it. With strained sight I gazed upon this monstrous death! Woe to those who are sucked in by that dreadful whirlpool, for there is no escape. The abyss has no bottom; destruction is sure to all who are caught in the tremendous down-rush! Even ships far out at sea on other tacks, though they escape this maelstrom, are hindered in their course by it, for this one monstrous devourer labors to absorb all and leaves no bay nor harbor nor foreign main unaffected by its perpetual draught. As I was thinking of this giant evil and wondering how I could navigate my own boat to avoid this mouth of hell, I saw a hand that had the mark of a nail upon its palm, and lo, it held a mighty magnet that attracted every vessel with a force greater than any born of sea or storm. This magnet attracted many ships so that they flew to it at once and were gently drawn toward their desired haven in the very teeth of the maelstrom. I saw other vessels in which the mariners hoisted sail to try to escape the influence of this magnet, and even put out their oars to strive to get away, and some of them did so escape. Alas, they floated farther and farther into the maelstrom's destructive power, to be sucked down to their perdition. These were so besotted that they labored against mercy and resolved to be destroyed. We are glad that all are not left to act so madly.

You must have seen an instance of drawing very often down in the river. A grand vessel is bound for the Indies, but how can it be taken down to The Nore? It is difficult to move the heavy craft. There it must lie. But here comes a steam-tug. The large vessel hands a rope on board the tug, and now the steam is up. Tug, tug, tug, the paddlewheels revolve, and the big ship begins to follow the lead. It is no longer motionless; it will soon be walking the waters as a thing of life. A pleasant sight—the tug draws it gently out to sea and then leaves it to pursue its distant voyage. Just so may Jesus draw you away from sinful pleasures and from self-righteousness.

What Does This Mean?

Well, it means this first—that *men, by nature, are a long way off from Christ.* You were not born converted. Of that, I am sure. Nor were you born a Christian either, and though they took you to the font and said that they made you a "member of Christ, a child of God, and an inheritor of the kingdom of heaven," there was not a word of truth in it. For you were such a child of God that you loved sin, such a member of Christ that you knew nothing of him, and such an inheritor of the kingdom of heaven that, unless God saves you, you will never get there. I may say of Christians who are made in that way, "They have mouths, but do not speak; eyes, but do not see. They have ears, but do not hear;   noses, but do not smell" (Ps. 115:5–6). And I fear that I must add, "Those who make them become like them; so do all who trust in them" (115:8). It is a poor Christianity that is created by such monstrous folly. "You must be born again," and you must be born again of the Spirit of God, or you cannot enter the kingdom of heaven. Man is a long way off from Christ, and Christ must draw him. Friend, ask him to draw you.

I gather another lesson—that *men will not come to Christ unless he draws them.* Sometimes, when I am trying to prepare a sermon to preach, I say to myself, "Why must I take all this trouble?" If men were in their senses, they would run to Christ without calling. Why must we put this business so temptingly? Why must we plead? Why must we be so earnest? Because men do not want to come, not even to their own Savior. They do not wish to have their sins forgiven. They do not wish to be renewed in heart. And they will never come—no, not one mother's son— unless he who sent Christ to them will draw them to Christ. A work of grace in the heart is absolutely necessary before the sacrifice of the Lord Jesus will be accepted by any one of us. Jesus said, "You refuse to come to me that you may have life" (John 5:40). What our Lord said is true to this hour—man has not improved an atom.

But then, learn another lesson. If there is any man here who Christ is drawing, he need not ask, "May I come?" Of course, you may, if you feel drawn to come. Are you coming? Come, and welcome. Christ never yet turned away a soul that came to him—not one. "Whoever comes to me I will never cast out" (John 6:37). If he is drawing you, run, for you have scriptural warrant for so doing. "Draw [us]: we will run after you" (Songs 1:4). If tonight you feel any kind of tugging at your heartstrings, do not hesitate a moment. Come along with you. When God draws, then, is your time to move. What do the sailors say? "There's a breeze, Jack. Aye, aye, boys, up with the anchor, now for every stitch of canvas, we can make headway now." Do you feel any kind of breeze? Is the breath of the Holy Spirit moving upon you in any degree? Do you feel inclined to say, "I will go to Jesus"? Then fly away with you, like a full-sailed ship before a fair wind. And by God's help may you soon make the port of everlasting salvation.

Let us finish up by saying that, if Christ has said that he will draw, then, he will draw tonight. The attractions of the Lord Jesus are continual. He draws, and he will always draw. He is drawing now. Do not pull back, lest his drawing should cease, and you should perish, but rather let your heart sing—

He drew me, and I followed on,
Charmed to confess the force divine.

Oh, Spirit of God, draw men to Jesus. This is the way of salvation; trust Christ and you are saved. Rely wholly on what Christ is and what he has done, and you are saved. In that very act there is a change effected within you that will show itself forever in your character, for he who believes in Jesus Christ, the Son of God, is born again. The faith that looks to Jesus and the life that lives upon Jesus come together. I cannot tell you which is first—the new birth or faith. Can you tell me which spoke of a wheel moves first? No. And these are spokes of one and the same wheel. "He who believes in him has everlasting life." Oh, believe him! Trust him. Lay hold upon him. Accept him, and go your way, and the mountains and the hills will break forth before you into singing, and all the trees of the field will clap their hands.

Amen. So, let it be!

The Tomb of Jesus

**No. 18, Exeter Hall, Strand, London, England,
April 8, 1855, Easter Morning**

Come, see the place where the Lord lay.
– Matthew 28:6

Every circumstance connected with the life of Christ is deeply interesting to the Christian mind. Wherever we behold our Savior, he is well worthy of our notice.

> His cross, his manger, and his crown,
> are big with glories yet unknown.

All his weary pilgrimage, from Bethlehem's manger to Calvary's cross, is in my eyes, paved with glory. Each spot upon which he trod is to our souls consecrated at once simply because there the foot of earth's Savior and our own Redeemer once was placed. When he comes to Calvary, the interest thickens, then our best thoughts are centered on him in the agonies of crucifixion. Nor does our deep affection permit us to leave him, even when, the struggle being over, he yields up the ghost. His body, when it is taken down from the tree, still is lovely in our eyes—we fondly linger around the motionless clay. By faith, we discern Joseph of Arimathea and the timid Nicodemus, assisted

161

by those holy women, drawing out the nails and taking down the mangled body. We behold them wrapping him in clean white linen, hastily girding him round with belts of spices, then putting him in his tomb and departing for the Sabbath rest.

We will, on this occasion, go where Mary went on the morning of the first day of the week, when waking from her couch before the dawn, she aroused herself to be early at the sepulcher of Jesus. We will try, if it be possible, by the help of God's Spirit, to go as she did—not in body but in soul—we will stand at that tomb. We will examine it, and we trust we will hear some truth-speaking voice coming from its hollow bosom, which will comfort and instruct us so that we may say of the grave of Jesus when we go away, "It was none other than the gate of heaven," a sacred place, deeply solemn, and sanctified by the slain body of our precious Savior.

An Invitation Given

I will commence my remarks this morning by inviting all Christians to come with me to the tomb of Jesus. "Come, see the place where the Lord lay." We will labor to render the place attractive. We will gently take your hand to guide you to it, and may it please our Master to make our hearts burn within us while we talk by the way.

Away, you profane, you souls whose life is laughter, folly, and mirth! Away, you sordid and carnal minds who have no taste for the spiritual, no delight in the celestial. We ask not your company. We speak to God's beloved, to the heirs of heaven, to the sanctified, the redeemed, the pure in heart, and we say to them, "Come, see the place where the Lord lay." Surely you need no argument to move your feet in the direction of the holy sepulcher. But still, we will use the utmost power to draw your spirit there. Come then, for 'tis the *shrine of greatness*, 'tis the resting place of *the man*, the Restorer of our race, the Conqueror of death and hell. Men will travel hundreds of miles to behold the place where a poet first breathed the air of earth. They will journey to the ancient tombs of mighty heroes or the graves of men renowned by fame. But where will the Christian go to find the grave of one so famous as was Jesus?

Ask me the greatest man who ever lived, and I tell you the Man Christ Jesus was "anointed with the oil of gladness above his fellows" (Heb. 1:9). If you seek a chamber honored as the resting place of genius, turn in here. If you would worship at the grave of holiness, come you here. If you would see the hallowed spot where the choicest bones that ever were fashioned lay for a while, come with me, Christian, to that quiet garden, hard by the walls of Jerusalem.

Come with me, moreover, because it is the *tomb of your best friend.* The Jews said of Mary, "She goes to his grave to weep there." You have lost your friends. Some of you have planted flowers on their tombs. You go and sit at eventide upon the green grass, bedewing the grass with your tears, for there your mother lies, and there your father, or your wife. Oh, in pensive sorrow come with me to this dark garden of our Savior's burial. Come to the grave of your best friend, your brother, yea, one who "sticks closer than a brother." Come, then, to the grave of your dearest relative, O Christian, for Jesus is your Husband; "your maker is your husband, the LORD of hosts is his name" (Isa. 54:5). Does not affection draw you? Do not the sweet lips of love woo you? Is not the place sanctified where one so well-beloved slept, although but for a moment? Surely you need no eloquence. If it were needed, I have none. I have but the power, in simple but earnest accents, to repeat the words, "Come, see the place where the Lord lay." On this Easter morning, pay a visit to his grave, for it is the grave of your best friend.

Yea, more, I will further urge you to this pious pilgrimage. *Come, for angels bid you.* Angels said, "Come, see the place where the Lord lay." The Syrian version reads, "Come, see the place where *our* Lord lay." Yes, angels put themselves with those poor women and used one common pronoun—*our.* Jesus is the Lord of angels as well as of men. You feeble women, you have called him Lord, you have washed his feet, you have provided for his wants, you have hung on his lips to catch his honeyed sentences, you have sat entranced beneath his mighty eloquence. You call him Master and Lord, and you do well. "But," said the seraph, "He is my Lord too." Bowing his head, he sweetly said, "Come, see the place where *our* Lord lay." Do not fear then, Christian, to step into that tomb. Do not dread to enter there, when the angel points with his finger and says, "Come, we will go together, angels and men, and see the royal bedchamber." You know that angels did go into his tomb, for they sat one at his head and the other at his foot in holy meditation. I picture to myself those bright cherubs sitting there talking to one another. One of them said, "It was there his feet lay," and the other replied, "And there his hands and there his head." And in celestial language did they talk concerning the deep things of God. Then they stooped and kissed the rocky floor, made sacred to the angels themselves, not because there they were redeemed but because there their Master and their Monarch, whose high commands they were obeying, did for a while, become the slave of death and the captive of destruction.

Come, Christian, then, for angels are the porters to unbar the door. Come, for a cherub is your messenger to usher you to the death-place of death himself. Nay, stare not from the entrance. Let not the darkness frighten you. The vault is not damp with the vapors of death, nor does the air contain anything of contagion. Come, for *it is a pure and healthy place*. Fear not to enter that tomb. I will admit that catacombs are not the places where we, who are full of joy, would love to go. There is something gloomy and repugnant about a vault. There are noxious smells of corruption. Oftentimes pestilence is born where a dead body has lain. But fear it not, Christian, for Christ was not left in hell, in Hades, neither did his body see corruption.

Come, there is no scent, yes, rather a perfume. Step in here, and if you did ever breathe the gales of Ceylon or winds from the groves of Araby, you will find them far excelled by that sweet holy fragrance left by the blessed body of Jesus, that alabaster vase that once held divinity and was rendered sweet and precious thereby. Do not think you will find anything obnoxious to your senses. Corruption never saw Jesus. No worms ever devoured his flesh. No rottenness ever entered into his bones. He saw no corruption. Three days he slumbered, but not long enough to putrefy. He soon arose, perfect as when he entered. Uninjured as when his limbs were composed for their slumber. Come then, Christian, summon up your thoughts, gather all your powers, here is a sweet invitation, let me press it again. Let me lead you by the hand of meditation, my brother. Let me take you by the arm of your fancy, and let me again say to you, "Come, see the place where the Lord lay."

There is yet one reason more why I would have you visit this Royal sepulcher: *because it is a quiet spot.* Oh, I have longed for rest, for I have heard this world's rumors in my ears so long that I have begged for "A lodge in some vast wilderness, some boundless contiguity of shade," where I might hide myself forever. I am sick of this tiring and trying life. My frame is weary; my soul is mad to repose itself awhile. I wish that I could lie myself down a little while by the edge of some pebbly brook, with no companion, save the fair flowers or the nodding willows. I wish that I could recline in stillness, where the air brings balm to the tormented brain, where there is no murmur save the hum of the summer bee, no whisper except that of the zephyrs, and no song except the caroling of the lark. I wish I could be at ease for a moment. I have become a man of the world; my brain is racked; my soul is tired. Oh! would you be quiet, Christian? Merchant, would you rest from your toils? Would you be calm for once, then come here? It is in a pleasant garden, far from the hum of Jerusalem. The noise and din of business will not reach you here. "Come, see the place where the Lord lay." It is a sweet resting spot, a withdrawing room for your soul, where you may brush your garments from the dust of earth and muse a while in peace.

Attention Requested

Thus, I have pressed the invitation, now we will enter the tomb. Let us examine it with deep attention, noticing every circumstance connected with it.

And first, mark that it is a *costly tomb*. It is no common grave. It is not an excavation dug out by the spade for a pauper in which to hide the last remains of his miserable and overwearied bones. It is a princely tomb. It was made of marble, cut in the side of a hill. Stand here, believer, and ask why Jesus had such a costly sepulcher. He had no elegant garments. He wore a coat without seam, woven from the top throughout, without an atom of embroidery. He owned no sumptuous palace, for he had nowhere to lay his head. His sandals were not rich with gold or studded with brilliants. He was poor.

Why, then, does he lie in a noble grave? We answer, for this reason: Christ was dishonored until he had finished his sufferings. Christ's body suffered contumely, shame, spitting, buffeting, and reproach, until he had completed his great work. He was trampled underfoot; he was "despised and rejected by men, a man of sorrows and acquainted with grief" (Isa. 53:3). But the moment he had finished his undertaking, God said, "No more shall that body be disgraced. If it is to sleep, let it slumber in an honorable grave. If it is to rest, let nobles bury it. Let Joseph, the councilor, and Nicodemus, the man of the Sanhedrin, be present at the funeral. Let the body be embalmed with precious spices; let it have honor. It has had enough of contumely, shame, reproach, and buffeting. Let it now be treated with respect." Christian, do you discern the meaning? Jesus, after he had finished his work, slept in a costly grave, for now his Father loved and honored him since his work was done.

But though it is a costly grave, *it is a borrowed one*. I see over the top of it, "Sacred to the memory of the family of Joseph of Arimathea." Yet Jesus slept there. Yes, he was buried in another's sepulcher. He who had no house of his own and rested in the habitation of other men. He who had no table but lived upon the hospitality of his disciples. He who borrowed boats in which to preach and had not anything in the wide world was obliged to have a tomb from charity.

Oh! should not the poor take courage? They dread to be buried at the expense of their neighbors, but if their poverty is unavoidable, why should they blush, since Jesus Christ himself was interred in another's grave? Ah! I wish I might have had Joseph's grave, to let Jesus be buried in it. Good Joseph thought he had cut it out for himself, and that he should lay his bones there. He had it excavated as a family vault, and lo, the Son of David makes it one of the tombs of the kings. But he did not lose it by lending it to the Lord; rather he had it back with precious interest. He only lent it three days, then Christ resigned it. He had not injured but perfumed and sanctified it and made it far more holy so that it would be an honor in the future to be buried there. It was a borrowed tomb. And why? I take it not to dishonor Christ but to show that as his sins were borrowed sins, so his burial was in a borrowed grave. Christ had no transgressions of his own. He took *ours* upon his head. He never committed a wrong, but he took all my sin and all yours, if you are believers. Concerning all his people, it is true, he bore their griefs and carried their sorrows in his own body on the tree. Therefore, as they were others' sins, so he rested in another's grave. As they were sins imputed, so only the grave was his by imputation. It was not his sepulcher; it was the tomb of Joseph.

Let us not weary in this pious investigation but with fixed attention observe everything connected with this holy spot. The grave, we observe, *was cut in a rock.* Why was this? The Rock of Ages was buried in a rock—a Rock within a rock. But why? Most persons suggest that it was so ordained that it might be clear that there was no covert way by which the disciples or others could enter and steal the body away. Very possibly it was the reason, but oh! my soul, can you not find a spiritual reason? Christ's sepulcher was cut in a rock. It was not cut in a mold that might be worn away by water or might crumble and fall into decay. The sepulcher stands, I believe, entire to this day. If it does not naturally, it does spiritually. The same sepulcher that took the sins of Paul will take my iniquities into its bosom. For if I ever lose my guilt, it must roll off my shoulders into the sepulcher. It was cut in a rock so that if a sinner were saved a thousand years ago, I too can be delivered, for it is a rocky sepulcher where sin was buried. It was a rocky sepulcher of marble where my crimes were laid forever—buried, never to have a resurrection.

You will mark, moreover, that tomb was one *wherein no other man had ever lain.* Christopher Ness says, "When Christ was born, he lay in a virgin's womb and when he died, he was placed in a virgin tomb. He slept where never man had slept before." The reason was that none might say that another person rose, for there never had been any other body there, thus a mistake of persons was impossible. Nor could it be said that some old prophet was interred in the place and that Christ rose because he had touched his bones. You remember when Elisha was buried, and as they were burying a man, behold he touched the prophet's bones and arose. Christ touched no prophet's bones, for none had ever slept there. It was a new chamber, where the Monarch of the earth did take his rest for three days and three nights.

We have learned a little, then, with attention, but let us stoop down once more before we leave the grave and notice something else. We see the grave, but do you *notice the grave clothe*s, all wrapped and laid in their places, the napkin being folded up by itself? Why are the grave clothes folded up? The Jews said robbers had abstracted the body, but if so, surely, they would have stolen the clothes. They would never have thought of folding them up and laying them down so carefully; they would be too much in haste to think of it. Why was it, then? To manifest to us that Christ did not come out in a hurried manner. He slept until the last moment, then he awoke. He came not in haste. They will not come out in haste, neither by flight, but at the appointed moment will his people come to him. So at the precise hour, the decreed instant, Jesus Christ leisurely awoke, took off his grave clothes, left them all behind him, and came forth in his pure and naked innocence, perhaps to show us that as clothes are the offspring of sin, when sin was atoned for by Christ. He left all raiment behind him, for garments are the badges of guilt. If we had not been guilty, we would never have needed them.

Then, the napkin, mark you, was laid by itself. The grave clothes were left behind for every departed Christian to wear. The bed of death is well-sheeted with the garments of Jesus, but the napkin was laid by itself because the Christian, when he dies, does not need that. It is used by the mourners and the mourners only. We will all wear grave-clothes, but we will not need the napkin. When our friends die, the napkin is laid aside for us to use, but do our ascended brothers and sisters use it? No, the Lord God has wiped away all tears from their eyes. We stand and view the corpses of the dear departed, we moisten their faces with our tears, letting whole showers of grief fall on their heads, but do *they* weep? Oh, no. Could they speak to us from the upper spheres, they would say, "Weep not for me, for I am glorified. Sorrow not for me. I have left a bad world behind me and have entered into a far better." They have no napkin, they weep not. Strange it is that those who endure death weep not, but those who see them die are weepers. When the child is born, it weeps when others smile (say the Arabs), and when it dies, it smiles while others weep. It is so with the Christian. O blessed thing! The napkin is laid by itself because Christians will never want to use it when they die.

Emotion Excited

We have thus surveyed the grave with deep attention, and I hope, with some profit to ourselves. But that is not all. I love a religion that consists, in a great measure, of emotion. Now, if I had power like a master, I would touch the strings of your hearts and fetch a glorious tune of solemn music from them, for this is a deeply solemn place into which I have conducted you.

First, I would bid you stand and see the place where the Lord lay with *emotions of deep sorrow*. Oh come, my beloved brother, your Jesus once lay there. He was a murdered man, my soul, and you the murderer.

> Ah, you, my sins, my cruel sins,
> His chief tormentors were,
> Each of my crimes became a nail,
> And unbelief the spear.
> Alas! and did my Savior bleed?
> And did my Sovereign die?

I slew him—this right hand struck the dagger to his heart. My deeds slew Christ. Alas! I slew my best beloved. I killed him who loved me with an everlasting love. You, eyes, why do you refuse to weep when you see Jesus's body mangled and torn? Oh! give rent to your sorrow, Christians, for you have good reason to do so. I believe in what Hare says, that there was a time in his experience when he could so sympathize with Christ that he felt more grief at the death of Christ than he did joy. It seemed so sad a thing that Christ should have to die, and to me it often appears too great a price for Jesus Christ to purchase worms with his own blood. I think I love him so much that if I had seen him about to suffer, I should have been as bad as Peter and have said, "Far be it from you, Lord!" But then he would have said to me, "Get behind me, Satan!" For he does not approve of that love that would stop him from dying. "Shall I not drink the cup that the Father has given me?" But I think had I seen him going up to his cross, I would gladly have pressed him back and said, "Oh! Jesus, You, must not die. I cannot have it. Will you purchase my life with a price so dear?" It seems too costly, for him who is the Prince of Life and Glory, to let his fair limbs be tortured in agony. That the hands that carried mercies should be pierced with accursed nails. That the temples that were always clothed with love should have cruel thorns driven through them. It appears too much. Oh! weep, Christian, and let your sorrow rise. Is not the price all but too great, that your Beloved should for you resign *himself?*

Oh! I should think if a person were saved from death by another, he would always feel deep grief if his deliverer lost his life in the attempt. I had a friend who, standing by the side of a piece of frozen water, saw a young lad in it and sprang upon the ice in order to save him. After clutching the boy, he held him in his hands and cried out, "Here he is! Here he is! I have saved him." But just as they caught hold of the boy, he sank himself, and his body was not found for some time afterward, when it was quite dead. Oh! it is so with Jesus. My soul was drowning. From heaven's high portals he saw me sinking in the depths of hell. He plunged in.

> He sank beneath his heavy woes,
> To raise me to a crown;
> There's never a gift his hand bestows,
> But cost his heart a groan.

Ah, we may indeed regret our sin, since it slew Jesus. Now, Christian, change your note a moment. "Come, see the place where the Lord lay," *with joy and gladness.* He does not lie there now. Weep when you see the tomb of Christ, but rejoice because it is empty. Your sin slew him, but his divinity raised him up. Your guilt has murdered him, but his righteousness has restored him. Oh! He has burst the bonds of death. He has taken off the grave clothes of the tomb and has come out more than conqueror, crushing death beneath his feet. Rejoice, O Christian, for he is not there—he is risen. "Come, see the place where the Lord lay."

One more thought, and then I will speak a little concerning the doctrines we may learn from this grave. "Come, see the place where the Lord lay" *with solemn awe,* for you and I will have to lay there too.

> Hark! From the tomb a doleful sound,
> My ears, attend the cry;
> You living men, come view the ground
> Where you must shortly lie.
> Princes, this clay must be your bed,
> In spite of all your powers;
> The tall, the wise, the reverend head,
> Must lie as low as ours.

It is a fact we do not often think of, that we will all be dead in a little while. I know that I am made of dust and not of iron. My bones are not brass, nor my sinews steel. In a little while my body must crumble back to its native elements. But do you ever try to picture yourself the moment of your dissolution? My friends, there are some of you who seldom realize how old you are, how near you are to death. One way of remembering our age is to see how much remains. Think how old eighty is, and then see how few years there are before you will get there. We should remember our frailty. Sometimes I have tried to think of the time of my departure. I do not know whether I will die a violent death or not, but I would to God that I might die suddenly, for sudden death is sudden glory. I would I might have such a blessed exit as Doctor Beaumont and die in my pulpit laying down my body with my charge, ceasing at once to work and live. But it is not mine to choose.

Suppose I lie lingering for weeks in the midst of pains and griefs and agonies? When that moment comes, that moment that is too solemn for my lips to speak of, when the spirit leaves the clay, let the physician put it off for weeks or years, as we say he does, though he does not—when that moment comes, oh, you lips, be dumb and profane not its solemnity. When death comes, how is the strong man bowed down? How does the mighty man fall? They may say they will not die, but there is no hope for them. They must yield; the arrow has gone home. I knew a man who was a wicked wretch, and I remember seeing him pace the floor of his bedroom, saying, "O God, I will not die, I will not die." When I begged him to lie on his bed, for he was dying, he said he could not die while he could walk, and he would walk until he did die. Ah! he expired in the utmost torments, always shrieking, "O God, I will not die." Oh! That moment, that last moment. See how clammy is the sweat upon the brow, how dry the tongue, how parched the lips. The man shuts his eyes and slumbers, then opens them again. And if he be a Christian, I can fancy he will say,

> Hark! They whisper: angels say
> Sister spirit, come away.
> What is this absorbs me quite—
> Steals my senses—shuts my sight—
> Drowns my spirit—draws my breath?
> Tell me, my soul, can this be death?

We know not when he is dying. One gentle sigh, and the spirit breaks away. We can scarcely say, "He is gone," before the ransomed spirit takes its mansion near the throne. Come to Christ's tomb then, for the silent vault must soon be your habitation. Come to Christ's grave, for you must slumber there. And even you, you sinners, for one moment I will ask you to come also because you must die as well as the rest of us. Your sins cannot keep you from the jaws of death. I say, sinner, I want you to look at Christ's sepulcher too, for when you die, it may have done you great good to think of it. You have heard of Queen Elizabeth crying out that she would give an empire for a single hour. Or have you read the despairing cry of the gentleman on board the *Arctic*, when it was going down, who shouted to the boat, "Come back! I will give you £30,000 if you will come and take me in." Ah! poor man. It was but little if he had thirty thousand worlds if he could thereby prolong his life. "Skin for skin. Yea, all that a man has will he give for his life." Some of you who laugh this morning, who came to spend a merry hour in this hall, will be dying, and then you will pray and crave for life, and shriek for another Sabbath day. Oh, how the Sabbaths you have wasted will walk like ghosts before you! Oh, how they will shake their snaky hair in your eyes! How will you be made to sorrow and weep because you wasted precious hours, which, when they are gone, are gone too far ever to be recalled. May God save you from the pangs of remorse.

Instruction Imparted

And now, Christian brethren, "Come, see the place where the Lord lay," to learn a doctrine or two. What did you see when you visited "the place where the Lord lay?" "He is not here, for he has risen!" The first thing you perceive, if you stand by his empty tomb, is *his divinity*. The dead in Christ will rise first at the resurrection, but he who rose first, their Leader, rose in a different fashion. They rise by imparted power. He rose by his own. He could not slumber in the grave because he was God. Death had no dominion over him. There is no better proof of Christ's divinity than that startling resurrection of his, when he rose from the grave by the glory of the Father. O Christian, your Jesus is God. His broad shoulders that hold you up are indeed divine. And here you have the best proof of it because he rose from the grave.

A second doctrine here taught well may charm you, if the Holy Spirit applies it with power. Behold this empty tomb, O true believer, for it is a sign of *your acquittal* and your full discharge. If Jesus had not paid the debt, he would never have risen from the grave. He would have lain there until this moment if he had not canceled the entire debt by satisfying eternal vengeance. Oh! beloved, is not that an overwhelming thought?

It is finished! It is finished! Hear the rising Savior cry.

The heavenly turnkey came. A bright angel stepped from heaven and rolled away the stone, but he would not have done so if Christ had not done all. He would have kept him there. He would have said, "Nay, nay, you are the sinner now. You have the sins of all your elect upon your shoulder, and I will not let you go free until you have paid the uttermost farthing." In his going free, I see my own discharge.

My Jesus' blood's my full discharge.

As a justified man, I have not a sin against me in God's book. If I were to turn over God's eternal book, I should see every debt of mine receipted and canceled.

> Here's pardon for transgressions past,
> It matters not how black their cast,
> And O, my soul, with wonder view
> For sins to come, here's pardon too.
> While through your blood absolved, I am
> From sin's tremendous curse and blame.

One more doctrine we learn, and with that we will conclude—*the doctrine of the resurrection.* Jesus rose, and as the Lord our Savior rose, so all his followers must rise. Die I must—this body must be a carnival for worms. It must be eaten by those tiny cannibals, and possibly it will be scattered from one portion of the earth to another. The constituent particles of this, my frame, will enter into plants, and from plants pass into animals and thus be carried into far distant realms. But at the blast of the archangel's trumpet, every separate atom of my body will find its fellow, like the bones lying in the valley of vision, though separated from one another, the moment God will speak, the bone will creep to its bone, then the flesh will come upon it. The four winds of heaven will blow, and the breath will return. So, let me die, let beasts devour me, let fire turn this body into gas and vapor; all its particles will yet again be restored. This very selfsame, actual body will stare up from its grave, glorified and made like Christ's body, yet still the same body, for God has said it. Christ's same body rose, so will mine.

O my soul, do you now dread to die? You will lose your partner body a little while, but you will be married again in heaven; soul and body will again be united before the throne of God. The grave—what is it? It is the bath in which the Christian puts the clothes of his body to have them washed and cleansed. Death— what is it? It is the waiting room where we robe ourselves for immortality. It is the place where the body, like Esther, bathes itself in spices, that it may be fit for the embrace of its Lord. Death is the gate of life. I will not fear to die, then, but will say,

> Shudder not to pass the stream
> Venture all your care on him
> Him, whose dying love and power
> Still'd its tossing, hush'd its roar;
> Safe is the expanded wave,
> Gentle as a summer's eve;
> Not one object of his care
> Ever suffer'd shipwreck there.

Come, view the place, then, with all-hallowed meditation, where the Lord lay. Spend this afternoon, my beloved brethren, in meditating upon it and very often go to Christ's grave both to weep and to rejoice. You, timid ones, do not be afraid to approach, for it is no vain thing to remember that timidity buried Christ. Faith would not have given him a funeral at all. Faith would have kept him above ground and would never have let him be buried, for it would have said it would be useless to bury Christ if he were to rise. Fear buried him. Nicodemus, the night disciple, and Joseph of Arimathea, secretly, for fear of the Jews, went and buried him. Therefore, you timid ones, you may go too. Ready-to-Halt, poor Fearing, and you, Mrs. Despondency and Much-afraid, go often there; it is your favorite haunt. There build a tabernacle. There abide. And often say to your heart, when you are in distress and sorrow, "Come, see the place where the Lord lay."

Sermon #10

No Tears in Heaven

No. 643, Metropolitan Tabernacle, Newington,
London, England,
August 6, 1865

And God will wipe away every tear from their eyes.
– Revelation 7:17

It is an ill thing to be always mourning, sighing, and complaining concerning the present. However dark it may be, we may surely recall some fond remembrances of the past. There were days of brightness; there were seasons of refreshing from the presence of the Lord. Be not slow to confess, O believing soul, that the Lord has been your help! And though now your burden is very heavy, you will find an addition to your strength in the thought of seasons long since past, when the Lord lightened your load and made your heart leap for joy. Yet more delightful will it be to expect the future. The night is dark, but the morning comes. Over the hills of darkness, the day breaks. It may be that the road is rough, but its end is almost in view. You have been clambering up the steep heights of Pisgah, and from its brow you may view your glorious heritage. True, the tomb is before you, but your Lord has snatched the sting from death, and the victory from the grave. Do not, O burdened spirit, confine yourself to the narrow miseries of the present hour, but let your eyes gaze with fondness upon the enjoyment of the past. View with equal ardor the infinite blessings of old eternity when you were not, but when God set you apart for himself and wrote your name in his Book of Life. Let your glance flash forward to the future eternity, the mercies that will be yours even here on earth, and the glories that are stored up for you beyond the skies. I will be well rewarded, this morning, if I should minister comfort to one heavy spirit by leading it to remember the glory that is yet to be revealed.

Coming to our text, we will observe, in the first place, that as God is to wipe away tears from the faces of the glorified, *we may well infer that their eyes will be filled with tears until then.* And in the second place, it is worthy of reflection, that as God never changes, *even now he is engaged in drying tears from his children's eyes.* And then, coming right into the heart of the text, we will dwell on the great truth of God, that *in heaven divine love removes all tears from the glorified;* and so we will close, by making some inquiry as to *whether or not we belong to that happy company.*

We Are Supposed to Have Tears Now

Our first subject of meditation in the inference that tears are to fill the eyes of believers until they enter the promised rest. There would be no need to wipe them away if there were none remaining. They come to the very gates of heaven weeping and accompanied by their two comrades, sorrow and sighing; the tears are dried, and sorrow and sighing flee away. The weeping willow grows not by the river of the water of life, but it is plentiful enough below; nor will we lose it until we change it for the palm branch of victory. Sorrow's dewdrop will never cease to fall until it is transformed into the pearl of everlasting bliss—

> The path of sorrow, and that path alone,
> Leads to the place where sorrow is unknown.

Religion brings deliverance from the curse but not exemption from trial. The ancients were accustomed to use bottles in which to catch the tears of mourners. I think I see three bottles filled with the tears of believers. The first is a *common bottle*, the ordinary bottle containing griefs incidental to all men, for believers suffer even as the rest of the race. *Physical pain*, by no means, spares the servants of God. Their nerves, blood vessels, limbs, and inward organs are as susceptible to disease as those of unregenerate men. Some of the choicest saints have lain longest on beds of sickness, and those who are dearest to the heart of God have felt the heaviest blows of the chastening rod. There are pains that, despite the efforts of patience, compel the tears to wet the cheeks. The human frame is capable of a fearful degree of agony, and there are few who, at some time or other, watered their couch with tears because of the acuteness of their pains.

Coupled with this are *the losses and crosses of daily life.* What Christian among you trades without occasional difficulties and serious losses? Have any of you a lot so easy that you have nothing to deplore? Are there no crosses at home? Are there no troubles abroad? Can you travel from the first of January to the last of December without feeling the weariness of the way? Have you no blighted field, no bad debt, no slandered name, no harsh word, no sick child, no suffering wife to bring before the Lord in weeping prayer? You must be an inhabitant of another planet if you have had no griefs, for man is born to trouble as the sparks fly upward! No ship can navigate the Atlantic of earth without meeting with storms—it is only upon the Pacific of heaven that all is calm forevermore. Believers must, through much tribulation, inherit the kingdom of heaven. "Trials must and will befall." *Death* contributes to our woes; the heirs of immortality are often summoned to gather around the tomb. Who has not lost a friend? If Jesus wept, do not expect that we will be without the tears of bereavement; the well-beloved Lazarus died, and so will our choicest friends. Parents will go before us, infants will be snatched from us, brothers and sisters will fall before the scythe of death. Impartial foe of all, you spare neither virtue nor vice, holiness nor sin; with equal foot you tread on the cherished loves of all!

The Christian also knows *disappointments* as bitter and as keen as other men. Judas betrays Christ, Ahithophel is a traitor to David. We have had our Ahithophels, and we may yet meet with our Judas. We have trusted in friends, and we have found their friendships fail. We have leaned on what seemed a staff, and it has pierced us like a spear. You cannot, dear friends, traverse the wilderness of this world without discovering that thorns and thistles grow plenteously in it, and that, step as you may, your feet must sometimes feel their power to wound. The sea of life is salt to all men. Clouds hover over every landscape. We may forget to laugh, but we will always know how to weep. As the saturated fleece must drip, so must the human race, cursed by the fall, weep out its frequent griefs.

I see before me *a second bottle*. It is *black and foul*, for it contains tears distilled by the force of the fires of sin. This bottle holds more than the first and is far more regularly filled. Sin is more frequently the mother of sorrow than all the other ills of life put together. Dear brethren, I am convinced that we endure more sorrow from our sins than from God's darkest providences. Mark our rebellious *lack of resignation*! When trouble comes, it is not the trial that makes us groan so much as our rebellion against it. It is true the ox goad is thrust into us, but we kick against it, and then it hurts us far more. Like men with naked feet, we kick against the pricks. We head our vessel against the stream of God's will, and then murmur because the waves beat violently upon us. An unsubdued will is like a maniac's hand that tears himself. The chastisements that come directly from our heavenly Father are never as hard to bear as the fretting and fuming of our un-humbled self-will. As the bird dashes against the wires of its cage and breaks its own wing, even so do we. If we would take the cross as our gracious Father gives it, it would not gall our shoulders, but since we revolt from it and loathe the burden, our shoulders grow raw and sore, and the load becomes intolerable. More submission, and we would have fewer tears.

There are the tears, too, of *wounded, injured pride*, and how hot and scalding they are! When a man has been ambitious and has failed, how he will weep instead of standing corrected or gathering up his courage for a wiser venture. When a friend has spoken slightingly of us or an enemy has accused us, how we have had to put our fingers to our hot eyelids to keep the tears from streaming out and have felt all the while as full of wretchedness as we well could be. Ah, these are cruel and wicked tears. God wipe them away from our eyes now! Certainly, he must do it before we will be able to enter heaven.

How numerous, too, are the tears of *unbelief*! We manufacture troubles for ourselves by anticipating future ills that may never come, or which, if they do come, may be like the clouds, all "big with mercy," and "breaking with blessings on our head." We get to supposing what we should do if such-and-such a thing occurred, which thing God has determined never will occur. We imagine ourselves in positions where providence never intends to place us, and so we feel a thousand trials in fearing one. That bottle, I say, ought never to carry within it a tear from a believer's eyes, and yet it has had whole floods poured into it. Oh, the wickedness of mistrust of God and the bitterness with which that distrust is made to curse itself. Unbelief makes a rod for its own back; distrust of God is its punishment. It brings such lack of rest, such care, such tribulation of spirit into the mind that he who loves himself and loves pleasure had better seek to walk by faith and not by sight.

Nor must I forget the scalding drops of *anger against our fellow men* and of petulance and irritation because we cannot have our way with them. These are black and horrid tears, as foul as the vaults of Tophet. May we be saved from such unholy tears.

Sometimes, too, there are streams that arise from *depressed spirits*—spirits desponding because we have neglected the means of divine grace and the God of grace. The consolations of God are small with us because we have been seldom in secret prayer; we have lived at a distance from the Most High and have fallen into a melancholy state of mind. I thank God there will never come another tear from our eyes into that bottle when eternal love will take us up to dwell with Jesus in his kingdom!

We would never overlook the *third bottle*, which is the true
crystal bottle into which holy tears may drop, tears like the *lach-
rymae Christi*, the tears of Jesus, so precious in the sight of God.
Even these will cease to flow in heaven. Tears of *repentance,* like
glistening dewdrops fresh from the skies, are stored in this bottle.
They are not of the earth; they come from heaven, and yet we
cannot carry them there with us. Good Rowland Hill used to say
repentance was such a sweet companion that the only regret he
would have in going to heaven was in leaving repentance behind
him, for he could not shed the tears of repentance there. Oh, to
weep for sin! It is so sweet a sorrow that I would wish to be a
constant weeper! Like a dripping well, my soul would always
drop with grief that I have offended my loving, tender, gracious
God. Tears for *Christ's injured honor and slightedness* glisten in
the crystal of our third bottle. When we hear Jesus's name blasphemed among men or see his cause driven back in the day of
battle, who will not weep? Who can restrain his lamentations?
Such tears are diamonds in Christ's esteem; blessed are the eyes
that are mines of such royal treasure. If I cannot win crowns, I
will at least give tears. If I cannot make men love my Master, yet
will I weep in secret places for the dishonor they do him. These
are holy drops, but they are all unknown in heaven. Tears of
sympathy are much esteemed by our Lord; when we "weep with
those who weep" we do well; these are never to be restrained this
side of the Jordan. Let them flow. The more of them, the better
for our spiritual health. Truly, when I think of the griefs of men,
and above all, when I have communion with my Savior in his
suffering, I want to cry with George Herbert:

> Come all you floods, you clouds, you rains,
>   Dwell in my eyes! My grief has need
> Of all the watery things that nature can produce!
> Let every vein suck up a river to supply my eyes,
>   My weary, weeping eyes, too dry for me,
>   Unless they get new conduits, fresh supplies,
>   And with my state agree.

It would be well to go to the very uttermost of weeping if
it were always of such a noble kind, as fellowship with Jesus

brings. Let us never cease from weeping over sinners as Jesus did over Jerusalem. Let us endeavor to snatch the firebrand from the flame and weep when we cannot accomplish our purpose.

These three receptacles of tears will always be more or less filled by us as long as we are here, but in heaven, the first bottle will not be needed for the wells of earth's grief will all be dried up and we will drink from living fountains of water unsalted by a tear. As for the second, we will have no depravity in our hearts, and so the black fountain will no longer yield its nauseous stream. And as for the third, there will be no place among celestial occupations for weeping even of the most holy kind. Until then, we must expect to share in human griefs, and instead of praying against them, let us ask that they may be sanctified to us—I mean, of course, those of the former sort. Let us pray that tribulation may work patience, and patience experience, and experience the hope that makes us not ashamed. Let us pray that as the sharp edge of the engraving tool is used upon us, it may only remove our filth and fashion us into images of our Lord and Master. Let us pray that the fire may consume nothing but the dross and that the floods may wash away nothing but defilement. May we thank God that though before we were afflicted we went astray, yet now, by his grace, we have kept his Word, and so will it be a blessed thing, a divinely wise thing, that we should tread the path of sorrow and reach the gates of heaven with teardrops glistening in our eyes.

Jesus Is the Great Tear Wiper

Our second point is that, even here, if we would have our tears wiped away, we cannot do better than return to our God. Jesus is the great tear wiper. Observe, brethren, that God can remove every vestige of grief from the hearts of his people *by granting them complete resignation to his will*. Our selfhood is the root of our sorrow. If self were perfectly conquered, it would be insignificant to us whether love ordained our pain or ease appointed us wealth or poverty. If our will were completely God's will, then pain itself would be attended with pleasure, and sorrow would yield us joy for Christ's sake. As one fire puts out another, so the master passion of love to God, and complete absorption in his sacred will, quenches the fire of human grief and sorrow. Hearty resignation puts so much honey in the cup of gall that the wormwood is forgotten. As death is swallowed up in victory, so is tribulation swallowed up in contentedness and delight in God.

He can also take away our tears *by compelling our minds to dwell with delight upon the end that all our trials are working to produce.* He can show us that they are working together for good, and as men of understanding, when we see that we will be essentially enriched by our losses, we will be content with them. When we see that the medicine is curing us of mortal sickness and that our sharpest pains are only saving us from pains far more terrible, then will we kiss the rod and sing in the midst of tribulation, "Sweet affliction!"—sweet affliction, since it yields such peaceable fruits of righteousness.

Moreover, he can take every tear from our eyes in the time of trial by shedding abroad the love of Jesus Christ in our hearts more plentifully. He can make it clear to us that Christ is afflicted in our affliction. He can indulge us with a delightful sense of the divine virtue that dwells in his sympathy and make us rejoice to be co-sufferers with the Angel of the Covenant. The Savior can make our hearts leap for joy by reassuring us that we are written on the palms of his hands and that we will be with him where he is. Sick beds become thrones and hovels ripen into palaces when Jesus is made sure to our souls! My brethren, the love of Christ, like a great flood, rolls over the most rugged rocks of afflictions—so high above them that we may float in perfect peace where others are a total wreck. The rage of the storm is all hushed when Christ is in the vessel. The waters saw you, O Christ! The waters saw you and were silent at the presence of their King!

The Lord can also take away all present sorrow and grief from us by providentially removing its cause. Providence is full of sweet surprises and unexpected turns. When the sea has ebbed its uttermost, it turns again and covers all the sand. When we think the dungeon is fast and that the bolt is rusted in, he can make the door fly open in a moment! When the river rolls deep and black before us, he can divide it with a word or bridge it with his hands. How often have you found it so in the past? As a pilgrim to Canaan, you have passed through the Red Sea, in which you once feared you would be drowned. The bitter wells of Marah were made sweet by God's presence. You fought the Amalekite, you went through the terrible wilderness, you passed by the place of the fiery serpents, and you have yet been kept alive. And so shall you be. As the clear shining comes after rain, so will peace succeed your trials. As the black clouds fly before the compelling power of the wind, so will the eternal God make your griefs to fly before the energy of his grace. The smoking furnace of trouble will be followed by the bright lamp of consolation.

Still, the surest method of getting rid of present tears is communion and fellowship with God. When I can creep under the wing of my dear God and nestle close to his bosom, let the world say what it will, let the devil roar as he pleases, and let my sins accuse and threaten as they may—I am safe, content, happy, peaceful, rejoicing—

> Let earth against my soul engage,
> And hellish dares be hurled;
> Now I can smile at Satan's rage,
> And face a frowning world.

To say, "My Father, God"; to put myself right into his hands and feel that I am safe there; to look up to him, though it is with tears in my eyes, and feel that he loves me; then to put my head right into his bosom as the prodigal did and sob my griefs out there into my Father's heart—oh, this is the death of grief and the life of all consolation! Is not Jehovah called the God of all comfort? You will find him so, beloved. He has been "our help in ages past." He is "our hope for years to come." If he had not been my help, then my soul would have perished utterly in the day of its weariness and its heaviness. Oh, I bear testimony for him this day that you cannot go to him and pour out your heart before him without finding a delightful solace! When your friends cannot wipe away the tears, when you, with your strongest reasoning and your boldest efforts, cannot compel yourself to resignation, when your heart beats high and seems as if it would burst with grief, then pour out your hearts before him! God *is* a refuge for us! He is our castle and high tower, our refuge and defense. Only go to him, and you will find that even here on earth God will wipe away all tears from your eyes!

The Removal of All Tears

Now we shall have to turn our thoughts to what is the real teaching of the text—namely, the removal of all tears from the blessed ones above. There are many reasons why glorified spirits cannot weep. These are well known to you, but let us just hint at them. *All outward causes of grief are gone.* They will never hear the toll of the death knell in heaven. The mattock and the shroud are unknown things there. The horrid thought of death never flits across an immortal spirit. They are never parted; the great meeting has taken place to part no more. Up yonder, they have no losses and crosses in business. "They serve God day and night in his temple." They know no broken friendships there. They have no ruined hearts, no blighted prospects. They know even as they are known, and they love even as they are loved. No pain can ever fall on them—as yet they have no bodies, but when their bodies will be raised from the grave, they will be spiritualized so that they will not be capable of grief. The tear glands will be plucked away; although much may be there that is human, at least the tear glands will be gone—they will have no need of that organ. Their bodies will be unsusceptible to grief. They will rejoice forever! Poverty, famine, distress, nakedness, peril, persecution, slander—all these will have ceased. "The sun shall not strike them, nor any scorching heat." "They shall hunger no more, neither thirst anymore," and therefore, well may their tears cease to flow.

Again, *all inward evils will have been removed by the perfect sanctification worked in them by the Holy Spirit.* No evil of heart, of unbelief in departing from the living God, will vex them in paradise; no suggestions of the archenemy will be met and assisted by the uprisings of iniquity within. They will never be led to think harshly of God, for their hearts will be all love. Sin will have no sweetness to them, for they will be perfectly purified from all depraved desires. There will be no lusts of the eyes, no lusts of the flesh, no pride of life to be snares to their feet. Sin is shut out, and they are shut in. They are forever blessed because they are without fault before the throne of God. What a heaven must it be to be without spot or wrinkle or any such thing! Well, may *they* cease to mourn who have ceased to sin!

All fear of change also has been forever shut out. They know that they are eternally secure. Saints on earth are fearful of falling. Some believers even dream of falling away; they think God will forsake them and that men will persecute and take them. No such fears can vex the blessed ones who view their Father's face. Countless cycles may revolve, but eternity will not be exhausted, and while it endures, their immortality and blessedness will co-exist with it. They dwell within a city that will never be stormed; they bask in a sun that will never set; they swim in a flood-tide that will never ebb; they drink of a river that will never dry up; they pluck fruit from a tree that will never be withered. Their blessedness knows not the thought, which would act like a canker at its heart, that it might, perhaps, pass away and cease to be. They cannot, therefore, weep because they are infallibly secure and certainly assured of their eternal blessedness.

Why should they weep when every desire is gratified? They cannot wish for anything they will not have. Eyes and ears, heart and hands, judgment, imagination, hope, desire, will—every faculty will be satisfied! All that their vast powers can wish, they will continually enjoy. Though "eye has not seen, nor ear heard . . . the things which God has prepared for them who love him," yet we know enough, by the revelation of the Spirit, to understand that they are supremely blessed. The joy of Christ, which is an infinite fullness of delight, is in them. They bathe themselves in the bottomless, shoreless sea of infinite beatitude!

Still, dear friends, this does not quite account for the fact that all tears are wiped from their eyes. I like better the text that tells us that *God* will do it. And I want you to think with me of fountains of tears that exist even in heaven so that the celestial ones must inevitably weep if God did not, by a perpetual miracle, take away their tears. It strikes me that if God himself did not interfere by a perpetual outflow of abundant consolations, the glorified would have very deep cause for weeping. You will say, "How is this?" Why, in the first place, if it were not for this, *what regrets they must have for their past sins.* The more holy a man is, the more he hates sin. It is a token of growth in sanctification not that repentance becomes less acute but that it becomes more and more deep. Surely, dear friends, when we will be made perfectly holy, we will have a greater hatred of sin! If on earth we could be perfectly holy, I think we would do little else than mourn to think that so foul, black, and venomous a thing as sin had ever stained us, and we would weep bitterly that we had ever offended such a good, gracious, tender, abundantly loving God. Why, the sight of Christ, "the Lamb in the midst of the throne," would make us remember the sins from which he purged us. The sight of our heavenly Father's perfection would be blinding to us if it were not that by some sacred means (which we know not) God wipes away all these tears from our eyes. And though we cannot but regret that we have sinned, yet perhaps we will know that sin has been made to glorify God by the overcoming power of almighty grace, that sin has been made to be a black foil, a sort of setting for the sparkling jewel of eternal, sovereign grace, and it may be that for this reason we shed no tears over our past lives. They sing, "Unto him who has loved us, and washed us from our sins in his blood," but they sing that heavenly song without a tear in their eyes. I cannot understand how this may be, for I know I could not do so as I now am—let this be the best reason that God has wiped away the tears from their eyes.

Again, do you not think, beloved, that the thought of the vast expense of shame and woe, which the Savior lavished for our redemption, must, in the natural order of things, be a constant source of grief? We sing sometimes that hymn that reminds us of the angelic song before the throne, and in one of its verses, the poet says,

> But when to Calvary they turn,
> Silent their harps abide;
> Suspended songs a moment mourn
> The God who loved and died.

Now that is natural and poetical, but it is not true, for you know very well that there are no suspended songs in heaven and that there is no mourning even over Christ, "who loved and died." It seems to me that if I were thoroughly spiritualized and in such a holy state as those are in heaven, I could not look at the Lamb without tears in my eyes. How could I think of those five wounds, that bloody sweat in Gethsemane, that cruel crowning with thorns in Gabbatha, that mockery and shame at Golgotha—how could I think of it without tears? How could I feel that he loved *me* and gave himself for *me,* without bursting into a passion of holy affection and sorrow? Tears seem to be the natural expression of such hallowed joy and grief—

> Love and grief my heart dividing,
> With my tears his feet I'll bathe.

I must think it would be so in heaven if it were not that by a glorious method, I know not how, God will wipe away even those tears from our eyes. Does it not need the interference of God to accomplish this wonder?

Is there not another cause for grief—namely, *wasted opportunities?* Beloved, when we once ascend to heaven, there will be no more feeding of Christ's hungry people; there will be no giving of drink to the thirsty; no visiting his sick ones or his imprisoned ones; no clothing of the naked. There will be no instructing the ignorant; no holding forth the Word of God among "a crooked and twisted generation." It has been often and truly said that if there could be regrets in heaven, those regrets would be that we have wasted so many opportunities of honoring Christ on earth—opportunities that will then be gone forever. Now in heaven their hearts are not steeled and hardened so that they can look back on sins of omission without sorrow. I believe there will be the tenderest form of conscience there—for perfect purity would not be consistent with any degree of hardness of heart. If they are sensitive and tender in heart, it is inevitable that they should look back with regret on the failures of the life below—unless some more mighty emotion should overwhelm that of contrition. I can say, beloved, if God would take me to heaven, this morning, if he did not come in and by a special act of his omnipotence dry up that fountain of tears, I would almost forget the glories of paradise in the midst of my own shame—shame that I have not preached more earnestly and have not prayed more fervently and labored more abundantly for Christ! That text, to which we heard a reference from a dear brother during the week, where Paul says, "For three years I did not cease night or day to admonish every one with tears," is a text that we cannot, any of us, read without blushes and tears. And in heaven, I think if I saw the apostle Paul, I must burst out in weeping if it were not for this text, which says that "God shall wipe away *all* tears"—and these among them. Who but the Almighty God could do this!

Perhaps, again, another source of tears may suggest itself to you—namely, *regrets in heaven for our mistakes and misrepresentations and unkindness toward other Christian brethren.* How surprised we will be to meet in heaven some whom we did not love on earth! We would not commune with them at the Lord's Table. We would not acknowledge that they were Christians at all! We looked at them suspiciously if we saw them in the street. We were jealous of all their operations. We suspected their zeal as being nothing better than rant, and we looked on their best exertions as having sinister motives at the bottom. We said many hard things and felt a great many more than we said. When we will see these unknown and unrecognized brethren in heaven, will not their presence naturally remind us of our offenses against Christian love and spiritual unity? I cannot suppose a perfect man looking at another perfect man without regretting that he ever ill-treated him—it seems to me to be the trait of a gentleman, a Christian, and of a perfectly sanctified man above all others, that he should regret having misunderstood, misconstrued, and misrepresented one who was as dear to Christ as himself. I am sure, as I go round among the saints in heaven, I cannot (in the natural order of things) help feeling, "I did not assist you as I ought to have done. I did not sympathize with you as I ought to have done. I spoke a hard word to you. I was estranged from you," and I think you would all have to feel the same—inevitably you must, if it were not that by some heavenly means—I know not how—the eternal God will so overshadow believers with the abundant bliss of his own self that even that *cause* of tears will be wiped away!

Has it never struck you, dear friends, that if you go to heaven and *see your dear children left behind unconverted*, it would naturally be a cause of sorrow? When my mother told me that if I perished, she would have to say, "Amen," to my condemnation, I knew it was true, and it sounded very terrible and had a good effect on my mind. But at the same time, I could not help thinking, "Well, you will be very different from what you are now," and I did not think she would be improved. I thought, "Well, I love to think of your weeping over me far better than to think of you as a perfect being, with a tearless eye, looking on the damnation of your own child." It really is a very terrible spectacle, the thought of a perfect being looking down upon hell, for instance, as Abraham did, and yet feeling no sorrow, for you will recollect that in the tones in which Abraham addressed the rich man, there is nothing of pity. There is not a single syllable that indicates any sympathy with him in his dreadful woes. One does not quite comprehend that perfect beings, God-like beings, beings full of love and everything that constitutes the glory of God's complete nature, should yet be unable to weep, even over hell itself. They cannot weep over their own children lost and ruined! Now, how is this? If you can tell me, I will be glad—for I cannot tell you. I do not believe that there will be one atom less tenderness, one fraction less amiability and love and sympathy—I believe there will be more—but that they will be in some way so refined and purified, that while compassion for suffering is there, detestation of sin will be there to balance it, and a state of complete equilibrium will be attained. Perfect acquiescence in the divine will is probably the secret of it, but it is not my business to guess. I do not know what handkerchief the Lord will use, but I know that he will wipe all tears away from their faces, and these tears among them.

Yet, once again, it seems to me that spirits before the throne taking, as they must do, a deep interest in everything that concerns the honor of the Lord Jesus Christ *must feel deeply grieved when they see the cause of truth imperiled and the kingdom of Christ, for a time, put back.* Think of Luther or Wycliffe or John Knox as they see the advances of popery just now. Take John Knox first, if you will. Think of him looking down and seeing cathedrals rising in Scotland, dedicated to the service of the pope and Satan. Oh, how the stern old man, even in glory, I think, would begin to shake, and the old lion would lash his sides once more and half wish that he could come down and pull the nests to pieces that the rooks might fly away. Think of Wycliffe looking down on this country where the gospel has been preached so many years and seeing monks in the Church of England. Seeing spring up in our national establishment everywhere, not *disguised* popery, as it was ten years ago, but stark naked popery, downright popery, that unblushingly talks about the "Catholic Church," and is not even Anglican any longer! What would Wycliffe say? Why, I think as he leans over the battlements of heaven, unless Wycliffe is mightily altered, and I cannot suppose he is (except for the better, and that would make him more tenderhearted and still more zealous for God), he must weep to think that England has gone back so far and that on the dial of Ahaz the sun has beat a retreat. I do not know how it is they do not weep in heaven, but they do not.

The souls under the altar cry, "How long? How long? How long?" There comes up a mighty intercession from those who were slaughtered in the days gone by for Christ—their prayer rises, "How long? How long? How long?" And God, as yet, does not avenge his own elect, though they cry day and night unto him. Yet that delay does not cost them a single tear. They feel so sure that the victory will come, they anticipate so much the more splendid triumph because of its delay, and therefore, they do both patiently hope and quietly wait to see the salvation of God. They know that, without us, they cannot be made perfect, and so they wait until we are taken up, that the whole company may be completed, and that then the soul may be dressed in its body and they may be perfected in their bliss—they wait, but they do not weep. They wait and they cry, but in their cry, no sorrow has a place. Now, I do not understand this.

It seems to me that the more I long for the coming of Christ, the more I long to see his kingdom extended, the more I will weep when things go wrong, when I see Christ blasphemed, his cross trampled in the mire, and the devil's kingdom established. But the reason is all in this: "*God* shall wipe away all tears from their eyes."

I thought I would just indicate to you why it says that God does it. It strikes me that these causes of tears could not be removed by an angel, could not be taken away by any form of spiritual enjoyment apart from the direct interposition of Almighty God. Think of all these things and wonder over them, and you will recall many other springs of grief that would have flowed freely if omnipotence had not dried them up completely. Then ask how it is that the saints do not weep and do not cry, and you cannot get any other answer than this—God has done it in a way unknown to us—forever taking away from them the power to weep.

We Will Be among the Happy Company

And now, beloved, will we be among this happy company? Here is the question, and the context enables us to answer it. "They have washed their robes and made them white in the blood of the Lamb." There is their character. "Therefore they are before the throne of God." The blood is a sacred argument for their being there, the precious blood. Observe, "They washed their robes." It was not merely their feet, their worst parts—but they washed their robes, their best parts. A man's robes are his most honored attire. He puts them on, and he does not mind our seeing his robes. There may be filthiness beneath, but the robes are generally the cleanest of all. But you see they washed even them. Now, it is the mark of a Christian that he not only goes to Christ to wash away his black sins but to wash his duties too. I would not pray a prayer unwashed with Jesus's blood. I would not like a hymn I have sung to go up to heaven—except it had first been bathed in his blood, if I would desire to be clothed with zeal as with a cloak. Yet I must wash the cloak in my Master's blood, though I would be sanctified by the Holy Spirit, and wear imparted righteousness as a raiment of needlework, yet I must wash even that in his blood.

What do you say, dear friends? Have you washed in his blood? The meaning of it is, *Have you trusted in the atoning sacrifice?* "Without shedding of blood there is no remission of sin." Have you taken Christ to be your all in all? Are you now depending on him? If so, out of deep distress you will yet ascend, leaning on your Beloved, to the throne of God, and to the bliss that awaits his chosen. But if not, "there is none other name," there is no other way. Your damnation will be as just as it will be sure. Christ is "the Way." But if you will not tread it, you will not reach the end. Christ is "the Truth," but if you will not believe him, you will not rejoice. Christ is "the Life," but if you will not receive him, you will abide among the dead and be cast out among the corrupt. From such a doom, may the Lord deliver us and give us a simple confidence in the divine work of the Redeemer, and to him will be the praise eternally. Amen.

Recent Titles from Free Grace Press

Christ Precious to Those Who Believe

John Fawectt

Written in 1799, Christ Precious to Those Who Believe: The preciousness of Jesus Christ, to those who believe—practically considered and improved by John Fawcett is a "minor spiritual classic of the eighteenth century that deserves to be better known.

On Your Heart: A Three-Year Devotional for Families

A.J. Genco

On Your Heart is a guide for family worship based on a three-year cycle. It provides both Scripture passages to read and discussions questions to ask for each of the nearly 1100 days in the cycle. At the end of three years, you and your family will have read through and discussed the entire Bible together.

Let the Little Children Come: Family Worship on Sundays (And the Other Six Days Too)

Scott Aniol

This is a book you can use every day of your child-raising years. Your children will be gone sooner than you think; if you use this book as your guide, you will be glad you did. Don't let the opportunity slip away.

– Scott Brown, Pastor, Hope Baptist Church, Wake Forest, NC; President, Church and Family Life

Christian Duties

Zenas Trivett

Christian Duties, originally entitled Plain Christian Duties Recommended, is an address Zenas Trivett gave at the establishment of a new Baptist congregation in 1791, in which he lays out the various responsibilities of a faithful member of a local church.

The Failure of Natural Theology: A Critical Appraisal of the
Philosophical Theology of Thomas Aquinas

Jeffrey D. Johnson

Johnson's scholarly but gracefully readable text shows that his intellect notwithstanding, Aquinas's mingled metaphysics, mixed methodology, and promotion of "divine immobility" merit strong caution. This is the book the church has needed on this subject. It is an urgent read by one of our best theologians.

—Dr. Owen Strachan

The Missionary Crisis: Five Dangers Plaguing Missions and How the
Church Can Be the Solution

Paul Snider

The Missionary Crisis confronts five dangers facing missionaries and the local churches that send them and gives biblical and practical instruction for missionaries, sending churches, and mission organizations. This book boldly approaches gentle correction for the missionary to reverse these five crises in their ministries. It challenges the local church to prepare and equip men and women for the high calling of missionary life.

Seven Thoughts Every Christian Ought to Think Every Day: Laying
a Foundation for a Life of Prayer

Jim Scott Orrick

Searching for great resources to disciple new believers can be like Goldilocks tasting porridge. Too difficult, and it frustrates; too fluffy, and it misleads. Jim Orrick has that much sought-after gift of taking deep truths and bringing the tray to the common man. When a book can be handed to an unbeliever for evangelism, read through with a new believer to disciple, worked through with the family for worship, and also delight the soul of the seasoned in Christ, it is a helpful book.

– Josh Lagrange, Church planter

Basic Christian Doctrines

Dr. Curt Daniel

Usually, other attempts to accomplish a work like this fall flat. Either the subjects are treated with far too much verbiage—thus unnecessarily lengthening the prose, or else easy enough to read but are much too elementary in content. Daniel,   however, deftly succeeds with both aims where many other writers do not.

– Dr. Lance Quinn
Executive Vice-President,
The Expositors Seminary, Jupiter, FL

The Gospel Made Clear to Children

Jennifer Adams

The highest recommendation I can give to this wonderful book is that I will be reading it over and over again to my children. It is rich in biblical doctrine and is an invaluable instrument to aid parents in teaching their children the glorious truths of "God in Christ" reconciling the world to Himself. I know of no other book that so clearly communicates the great doctrines of the gospel to children.

– Paul Washer,
Author, Director of HeartCry Missionary Society

GRACE BIBLE
THEOLOGICAL
SEMINARY

Interested in becoming a student
or supporting our ministry?
Please visit gbtseminary.org